FILM REMAKES AND FRANCHISES

QUICK TAKES: MOVIES AND POPULAR CULTURE

Quick Takes: Movies and Popular Culture is a series offering succinct overviews and high-quality writing on cutting-edge themes and issues in film studies. Authors offer both fresh perspectives on new areas of inquiry and original takes on established topics.

SERIES EDITORS:

Gwendolyn Audrey Foster is the Willa Cather Professor of English and she teaches film studies in the Department of English at the University of Nebraska, Lincoln.

Wheeler Winston Dixon is the James Ryan Endowed Professor of Film Studies and Professor of English at the University of Nebraska, Lincoln.

Steven Gerrard, *The Modern British Horror Film*
Daniel Herbert, *Film Remakes and Franchises*
Ian Olney, *Zombie Cinema*
Valérie Orlando, *New African Cinema*
Steven Shaviro, *Digital Music Videos*
David Sterritt, *Rock 'n' Roll Movies*
John Wills, *Disney Culture*

Film Remakes and Franchises

DANIEL HERBERT

RUTGERS UNIVERSITY PRESS

New Brunswick, Camden, and Newark, New Jersey, and London

Library of Congress Cataloging-in-Publication Data
Names: Herbert, Daniel, 1974– author.
Title: Film remakes and franchises / Daniel Herbert.
Description: New Brunswick : Rutgers University Press, 2017. |
Series: Quick takes: movies and popular culture | Includes index.
Identifiers: LCCN 2017011520 (print) | LCCN 2017027573 (ebook) |
ISBN 9780813579429 (Epub) | ISBN 9780813579436 (Web PDF) |
ISBN 9780813590066 (cloth : alk. paper) |
ISBN 9780813579412 (pbk. : alk. paper)
Subjects: LCSH: Film remakes—History and criticism.
Classification: LCC PN1995.9.R45 (ebook) |
LCC PN1995.9.R45 H43 2017 (print) | DDC 791.43/6—dc23
LC record available at https://lccn.loc.gov/2017011520

A British Cataloging-in-Publication record for this book is
available from the British Library.

∞ The paper used in this publication meets the requirements
of the American National Standard for Information Sciences—
Permanence of Paper for Printed Library Materials, ANSI
Z39.48-1992.

Visit our website: www.rutgersuniversitypress.org

Manufactured in the United States of America

FOR ANNA, ONCE AGAIN. ANYTHING CAN BE REMADE.

CONTENTS

FILM REMAKES AND FRANCHISES

INTRODUCTION

Industrial Intertextuality and
The Force Awakens

At first (and second) glance, contemporary cinema seems incredibly unoriginal. Everywhere we look, there appears to be an endless flood of remakes, sequels, reboots, and franchises. It seems as though Hollywood produces only movies and television programs with recycled stories, characters, and imagery. Moreover, these images and characters appear again and again in a variety of other consumer merchandise, like toys and clothing. The situation is so remarkable yet commonplace that in October 2015 the parody news website The Onion published a story mocking the lack of originality in Hollywood. It stated that the Motion Picture Association of America (MPAA), the trade group that represents the major Hollywood studios, had instituted a new rating, "O," for "Original." It noted that this rating would "alert audiences of movies that are not based on existing works . . . [and] inform viewers that a particular film contains characters with whom they are unfamiliar, previously unseen set-tings, and novel plots" ("MPAA Adds New Rating"). The logic of this rating, as indicated in the story, was to keep moviegoers from feeling disturbed by the strain of seeing and thinking about something new. And the story asserted that "while audiences have reportedly been receptive to the new rating, directors and distributors have already decried it as severely damaging in regard to box-office revenues" ("MPAA Adds New Rating").

However hyperbolic and satirical this story may be, it points to genuine concerns regarding contemporary media. In its reversed sort of way, this Onion article sug-gests that contemporary viewers attend the movies in a ritualized, repetitive way in order to gain a sense of plea-sure and comfort through familiarity. Further, the story points out that the Hollywood studios are quite literally invested in producing content that recycles existing mate-rial. That is to say, even though this story mocks contem-porary movie fans as well as Hollywood, it also suggests that cinematic recycling occurs due to social, cultural desires as well as economic and industrial pressures.

We can see the validity of these concerns by looking at some articles that are *not* fictional. For instance, a review of the remake of *Cabin Fever* (2016) on the movie fan web-site Ain't It Cool News criticized the film in ways that are typical of many assessments of film remakes. The author invoked movie audiences by asserting, "remakes are a touchy subjects [*sic*] among film nerds," and then allowed that "films can be updated for a new generation, spun in a new way to make them relevant to the modern era, . . . and if they suck . . . they disappear from public consciousness and we don't really have to talk about them anymore" (Horrorella). Yet the writer continues by saying, "So what does this new version [of *Cabin Fever*] bring to the table? Absolutely . . . nothing." She concludes by writing, "The only way this waste of a film has a chance of flying is if we later learn that it was secretly some sort of commentary on the state of remake culture within the film community, and the necessity of original storytelling" (Horrorella).

Movie fans or film critics are not the only ones with concerns about the lack of original content coming out of Hollywood. This is a major issue within Hollywood itself, as movie producers and distributors continually assess what might be economically successful and strategize as to how they might best exploit the characters, stories, and brands under their ownership. A story appearing in September 2015 on the industry trade website Deadline Hollywood indicated that sixteen of the twenty highest-grossing films of that year were "retreads," such as *The Hunger Games: Mockingjay—Part 2* (2015), and noted further that "the retread group could set a record by accounting for 44% of the ultimate worldwide box office revenue for this year's top 20 releases" (Lieberman). Although these figures may simply confirm what we all suspect, namely, that remakes, sequels, and franchises earn vast fortunes for the Hollywood studios, this story also signaled some concern about this phenomenon. It quoted financial research analyst Vasily Karasyov as saying that "box office sales for films based on sequels, spinoffs and other forms of pre-existing intellectual properties such as comic books have 'played out'" and that Hollywood faces being "at the tail end of the process" of exploiting such material (Lieberman). In this regard, the story admits that franchises do, in fact, make an enormous amount of money but warns that Hollywood should prepare for this to not always be the case and, implicitly, suggests that movie producers would be wise to begin generating more new, original content.

Taken together, these stories from The Onion, Ain't It Cool News, and Deadline Hollywood indicate some of the major themes of this book. *Film Remakes and Franchises* examines many different forms of borrowing and recycling that characterize so much of contemporary cinema. By looking closely at film remakes and franchises, it is possible to see some of the most interesting, complex, and important forces that shape movie culture. Remakes and franchises constitute a significant amount of contemporary media production, and they are also prominent categories that audiences use to understand so much of the media they consume. Indeed, film remakes and franchises get defined as texts and as categories for understanding media products through a cultural process that entails multiple groups, including movie producers, distributors, advertisers, movie audiences, and fans—and film critics and scholars too.

To put it another way, remakes and franchises function as "cultural categories," in the sense that Jason Mittell has used that phrase to refer to genres (1, 11). As Mittell writes, "genre is best understood as a process of categorization that is not found within media texts, but operates across the cultural realms of media industries, audiences, policy, critics, and historical context" (xii). Although Mittell is specifically focused on "genre," this proposition also proves useful for thinking about a wide array of textual groupings and relationships, like remakes and franchises. The very notions of film remakes and franchises have been defined by different constituencies in a shared cultural discourse and, in this process, signify important struggles over cultural values. As these ideas and definitions relate to particular media forms, it is important to remain attentive to the formal features and textual elements that make certain films "remakes" or part of a "franchise." As Mittell indicates, "media texts function as important locales of generic discourses and must be examined on par with other sites, such as audience and industrial practices" (14). If cultural categories are constructed through discourses, then we should also hold to the idea that *films themselves* contribute significantly to public discourse and the shape of culture overall. This is as true of remakes and franchises as of any other cultural category.

Of course, "culture" and "discourse" are defined by contests for meaning and power, and the creation of a coherent cultural category, such as "the remake," can often be messy. There are many questions we can ask about remakes and franchises, and some of them might even seem to oppose one another. Are remakes simply products of crass commercialism, offering nothing in the way of creativity or artistry? Or are they opportunities for filmmakers to improve on narratives and characters, which get adapted to new historical and cultural contexts? And what do remakes and franchises say about film audiences? Do we enjoy them because we live in a culture of conformity? Or do we approach remakes, sequels, reboots, and franchise films as a kind of game, watching for references to older films and twists on known stories? It seems to me that none of these questions necessarily cancels out the others. Rather, remakes and franchises might function in all of these ways—and more.

Although this book does not provide a strictly historical account of film remakes and franchises, we should understand that these types of media are shaped by concrete historical circumstances, just like any other artistic practice or cultural category. Through an examination of several illustrative cases from throughout the history of cinema, we can see just how venerable and dynamic cinematic recycling truly is. Further, by looking at more contemporary examples, we will see how historical and cultural conditions weigh on the ways in which remakes, reboots, and franchise films are made, circulated, and consumed in our present moment; indeed, the categories "reboot" and "franchise" are themselves quite contemporary ways of defining films and related media. That is to say, our understandings of film remakes and franchises are shaped by our current historical circumstances, and these circumstances are the result of a long historical process.

Along these lines, it is worth noting that an article in the *New York Times* had resident film critics A. O. Scott and Manohla Dargis singing the praises of some of 2015's best films, in which they included several remakes, reboots, and major franchise films. Scott called *Mad Max: Fury Road* (2015) "a bloody, noisy chunk of manna from movie heaven" (Dargis and Scott). He also praised *Creed* (2015) and stated that it was "a near remake of the first [*Rocky*] movie that revised its hoary pugilistic themes and brought them into the present" (Dargis and Scott). Dargis engaged with the biggest film of the year, and the biggest franchise film to date, *Star Wars: The Force Awakens* (2015). Noting its remarkable critical, popular, and commercial success, she called the film "a collective bliss out" (Dargis and Scott). She then noted, "Some of this is just relief that at long last, a sequel isn't an abomination," thereby evoking the sense that film serials are generally bad, raising *The Force Awakens* above the rest of this type of film and, in fact, indirectly praising the film specifically *as* a sequel.

We might agree that *Fury Road*, *Creed*, and *The Force Awakens* are all good films. Each one draws from the history of a durable film franchise and successfully, and creatively, extends that franchise for contemporary audiences. *The Force Awakens*, in particular, has been singularly successful; the film has made more than $900 million in North America and $2 billion worldwide, making it the most successful film in the United States and the third-most successful film in the world at the time of this writing. We might see the success of *The Force Awakens* as indicating a widespread acceptance of everything the film represents, a general public acknowledgment and approval of the way it contributes to the *Star Wars* universe and to popular culture more generally. Yet we should remember that most films (including sequels and franchises) do not succeed and that the success of *The Force Awakens* was strategically planned through a deluge of advertising and promotional materials and, in fact, through this movie's calculated textual connectivity to other films, programs, books, and other texts within the *Star Wars* universe. Whatever it may represent, *Star Wars: The Force Awakens* raises many of the most important questions and problems regarding film remakes and franchises in contemporary culture. Indeed, this film, and the discussions around it, illustrates many key issues regarding film remakes and franchises in general.

As already noted, *The Force Awakens* was a financial as well as a critical success. Taking these two factors into consideration, we can therefore see the film, broadly, as an *industrial* success, which is to say that the movie made a lot of money, leading Disney, the company that made the film, to follow through with plans to create additional films—and television programs, toys, video games, and so on—based on this same property. Of course, *The Force Awakens* did not appear out of a vacuum, as *Star Wars* has been an immensely popular story world since the first film appeared in 1977. *The Force Awakens*, therefore, must also be considered in light of all the previous films, programs, comic books, and other related cultural texts that came before it. This one film is, in a very clear way, *intertextual*, meaning that it is deeply referential and connected to a huge number of other, previously existing cultural texts. If we think of these two factors together, then we can understand *The Force Awakens* as an industrial intertext. It is a cultural product designed to make money (industry), and it is simultaneously connected to a wide range of existing products (intertextuality).

Disney was able to produce this industrial intertext because the company owned the copyright to *Star Wars*. Although George Lucas created *Star Wars* in the 1970s and his company Lucasfilm had created innumerable *Star Wars* texts and products since that time, or allowed other companies to do so through the legal and economic process of licensing, Lucas sold the intellectual property rights for everything related to *Star Wars* to Disney in late 2012 for just over $4 billion. According to US copyright law, this authorizes Disney, and only Disney, to produce and sell cultural texts, in any medium, about *Star Wars*. And this is precisely the means by which a person or company can create industrial intertexts. Although we all have *ideas* about *Star Wars*, thus making it part of our minds and shared culture, intellectual property law gives specific people or companies the exclusive right to produce works related to those ideas and sell them for profit. Anyone can think about and have ideas about *Star Wars*, but only Disney can make money from those ideas.

The law states that copyright protects "original works of authorship fixed in any tangible medium of expression"

(Section 102), but as is so often the case, the use of the term "original" here is troublesome. Just how "original" is *The Force Awakens*? The film necessarily builds on the existing *Star Wars* idea and property. As soon as the sale of *Star Wars* was announced, it was also reported that Disney had outlines for three new films (Cieply), and another story reported that the company would begin production on these new movies immediately (Zeitchik). Thus, Disney prepared to make a new trilogy, or a set of three films that are linked by depicting the same characters in one overall continuous story. But, the story stated, this film would also be the seventh in a series (Zeitchik), a term for films or other texts that tell ongoing, continuous stories in the same diegesis or story world, without indicating when that story may end; hypothetically, a series can go on forever. And Manohla Dargis complicated the situation even more when she referred to *The Force Awakens* as a "sequel," which typically means a second film in a series or more generally can mean any film that continues the story of a previous film (Dargis and Scott).

From the start, then, *The Force Awakens* was blatantly unoriginal, in the sense that it was directly connected to and would openly draw from existing ideas and stories. In fact, some critics and fans noted a particularly striking resemblance between *The Force Awakens* and the "original" film, *Episode IV: A New Hope*. More pointedly, some critics referred to *The Force Awakens* as a "remake" of *A New Hope*, in this case meaning that this film repeated a substantial portion of the narrative of the previous film. This is an understandable assertion. In both *A New Hope* and *The Force Awakens*, we see a hero hide a crucial secret within a robot, or "droid," and this droid then wanders across a desert landscape in a journey to get this secret into the right hands. In both films, the protagonist, who lives on this desert planet, discovers the droid and commits to assisting in its journey. In both films, a heavy-breathing, masked villain hunts for this same secret in this droid and comes into conflict with the protagonist and the other heroes along the way. In both films, the enemies have an enormous superweapon capable of destroying planets, which the heroes attack in jet-fighter spaceships and destroy just before the weapon discharges. These are just some of the most obvious commonalities; there are many, many more.

Still others referred to *The Force Awakens* not as a remake but rather as a "reboot" (Thompson), a term that has been used increasingly since the early 2000s to describe certain films and other cultural texts. Generally, this means a film starts fresh and resets a narrative back to a (new) beginning. In the case of *The Force Awakens*, however, we see that this term is more complicated than simply describing a narrative. In this case, the reboot works industrially and culturally to refresh and restart a media franchise. Although financially successful, the prequel films, *The Phantom Menace* (1999), *Attack of the Clones* (2002), and *Revenge of the Sith* (2005), which told stories occurring before the events of the "Original Trilogy," were largely treated by fans as disappointing. When Disney first bought Lucasfilm in 2012, one report noted that there had been "a tension between fans over the direction of the series, with many reacting to Tuesday's news online by saying that the franchise needs a wholesale reinvention" (Zeitchik). Thus, *The Force Awakens* was intended not to rewrite or undo any of the previous films' stories but rather was burdened with the task of reinstilling widespread popular excitement for the very idea of *Star Wars*, thereby making it possible for Disney to produce additional products based on this intellectual property with confidence.

Indeed, *The Force Awakens* may be a single film, but it held the responsibility of representing and supporting an entire media franchise. Within the logic of a franchise, a specific intellectual property gets manifested as multiple consumer products, from movies and television programs to books, comic books, toys, video games, clothing, and so on. Franchises are generative, as franchise logic dictates that a copyright holder exploits that copyright in myriad ways, spreading a single property as far and wide as is profitable. So 2015 saw new *Star Wars* action figures, stuffed animals, and backpacks, among many other items and products, based on elements from *The Force Awakens*. However, franchise logic is not only about a single company exploiting a single idea but also entails a certain kind of industrial and cultural openness, or "sharing" (Johnson 16–17). With regard to *Star Wars* and *The Force Awakens*, we can see the industrial side to this openness in the fact that Disney has allowed, for a fee, a number of other companies to produce *Star Wars*–related products. The novelization for *The Force Awakens*, for instance, was published by Del Rey, an imprint of Penguin Random House (Trachtenberg and Fritz), while the video game *Star Wars: Battlefront*, which includes elements seen in *The Force Awakens*, was produced by Electronic Arts Inc. (Van Der Lind).

In this manner, multiple companies are capable of making use of the *Star Wars* copyright, making the franchise somewhat industrially open or *inclusive*. Another aspect to the inclusiveness of media franchises is the manner in which they aim to engage with multiple, sometimes disparate and sometimes overlapping, groups of consumers. That is to say, franchises generate different products based on the same idea or copyright specifically designed to engage different kinds of people, making franchises socially or culturally inclusive to some degree. We see stuffed animals for toddlers, action figures for older children, ornate models for adult collectors, video games for gamers, novels for teen and adult readers, and the movie *The Force Awakens* for everyone. Although Disney imagines all these different groups in terms of their ability to consume commercial products, that is, as consumers in a consumer society, by producing this wide array of *Star Wars* material, the company facilitates different groups' participation in popular culture.

A truly remarkable aspect of *The Force Awakens*, particularly as a globally popular and financially successful film, is that it features a comparatively socially diverse cast. The film's protagonist, Rey, is played by a woman, Daisy Ridley, and her fellow heroes, Finn and Poe Dameron, played by John Boyega and Oscar Isaac, are Black and Latino, respectively. Certainly, we still have white men in heroic, lead roles, like Harrison Ford as Han Solo and Mark Hamill as Luke Skywalker. Moreover, the science-fiction setting of this film allows it to represent people of different genders, races, and ethnicities and yet ignore how "gender," "race," and "ethnicity" occur as social and cultural identities and the frequently fraught matter in which they are constructed and experienced. Along these lines, Kristen Warner has pointedly analyzed how media representations of "race" can follow a problematic ideology of "colorblindness" (7–12). Warner shows how this ideology informs the industrial practice of "blindcasting," or casting actors of diverse racial identities in roles that are "racially neutral," which allows writers "to avoid explicitly writing race into the script" and allows media producers to avoid the cultural specificities of race (13). Yet, although this issue appears relevant to *The Force Awakens*, it still seems conspicuous and impressive to me that none of the new characters, who are now central to the *Star Wars* franchise, conform to the stereotypical model for action-cinema heroes. There is important social diversity behind the scenes of *The Force Awakens* as well. Although the director of the film, J. J. Abrams, is a white man, Disney hired a woman, Kathleen Kennedy, to run Lucasfilm, and she has been a prominent public face in promoting *The Force Awakens* and the *Star Wars* franchise more generally.

Multiple news articles made positive comments about the film's casting. One story, titled "With Diverse Characters, 'The Force Awakens' Has Great Success While Practicing Inclusive Casting," said that the choice of actors for this film was "a step in the right direction," especially when compared with the previous *Star Wars* films (Kirst). Another story credited the film with showing that "it is not only white males who get to harness the power of the Force" (Keegan). Even more positively, and inclusively, the author wrote, "When Finn grasps a lightsaber, it's a cue to *anyone* in the audience who feels like an outsider in the culture—the power of adventure lives within you too" (Keegan; emphasis added). Here, the franchise logic of industrial and cultural inclusion aligns in a rather profound way with the social inclusiveness of the text itself. If *The Force Awakens* truly does remake *A New Hope*, then it does so in a way that better engages with the complex, multifaceted, socially and cultural diverse world in which we currently live. And while social diversity is not necessarily intrinsic to reboots, remakes, or franchises, it is an important aspect of contemporary media that merits serious consideration.

More broadly, *Film Remakes and Franchises* provides the means to seriously consider these important cultural forms as well as provides insights into some notable case studies. As we saw in the case of *The Force Awakens*, there are many names and categories for understanding the many forms of intertextuality we see in contemporary media culture. Accordingly, it is important to survey, define, and explore these categories, including the remake, the reboot, and the franchise, as well as related terms such as "adaptation" and "parody," which is the goal of chapter 1. Film remakes, which are the focus of chapter 2, represent a particularly troublesome category. Consistently, remakes have been critically disregarded even while movie producers have continuously made them. But arguing whether remakes are "good" or "bad" seems to be an intellectual dead end. Instead, by looking at a wide range of examples, including some early films by Thomas Edison, *You've Got Mail* (1998), and *Dr. Jekyll and Mr. Hyde* (1920, 1931, 1941), we can understand the very processes through which remakes get defined in different contexts. One cannot simply look at an original film and a remake to understand them, but we must also look at other movies, television programs, and other cultural texts to understand why remakes appear the way they do.

As noted earlier, franchises expand well beyond cinema and entail the use of characters, imagery, and stories across multiple media and also as countless forms of consumer merchandise. Further, franchises regularly seek out multiple audiences through these different texts and products, addressing multiple social groups as they attempt to spread a brand as far as possible. Thus, although globally popular franchises such as *The Avengers* or *Star Wars* are certainly important to understanding contemporary media, chapter 3 details how media franchises can engage with issues of social diversity. Cases such as *Daniel Tiger's Neighborhood, Paranormal Activity,* and *Sex and the City* demonstrate how media franchises are able to "enfranchise" different social groups, if only to the extent that they provide opportunities for groups to engage meaningfully with popular culture.

We might ultimately ask what it means, in the present historical moment and social context, that so much of culture is repetitive and commercialized. Remakes and franchises are big business. But they are also big culture. What are we to make of the fact that so much of our time, energy, thought, and sense of identity—and money—get wrapped up in a somewhat limited number of ideas, stories, and characters, which are owned by a *severely* limited number of corporations? Film remakes and franchises point toward the complex and contentious way in which popular culture gets made, circulated, and consumed. *Film Remakes and Franchises* aims to show just how complex and interesting this process is.

1

COMING TO TERMS
WITH INTERTEXTUALITY

Nothing is original. All of culture comes from the culture
before it, and every cultural text or work of art borrows
from previous texts and works of art. Think of it this way:
All of the language you use in your everyday life may
be "original," in the sense that you are saying words and
phrases spontaneously, in a spur-of-the-moment and
improvisational way. Each time you speak, you say something new and original within that context. But you did
not invent language. It was given to you and taught to you
by family, teachers, and everyone else you have come into
contact with. Nothing you say or write is truly "original,"
as the words you use and ways in which you structure
your sentences ultimately come from outside you, from
before you ever spoke or wrote anything.

  Cultural texts work in a similar way. Indeed, it is this
very sense that art and culture are unoriginal that leads us

to use the word "text" to describe cultural products. Critic and theorist Roland Barthes made this distinction in an essay called "From Work to Text." There, he asserted that it is less accurate to think of cultural artifacts as discrete objects, or "works," than to approach art and culture as made up of "texts," which are interconnected with existing texts. Barthes wrote that every text is "woven entirely with citations, references, echoes, cultural languages (what language is not?), antecedent or contemporary, which cut across it through and through in a vast stereophony. The intertextual in which every text is held, it itself being the text-between of another text, is not to be confused with some origin of the text" (160). By setting aside the notion of originality, we can perhaps better appreciate the ways in which cultural texts remain interesting or meaningful despite the fact that all of them are, in various ways, highly repetitive.

In fact, the idea of copying and imitation within the arts has not always had a negative connotation, in a wide variety of contexts. With theatrical plays or symphonies, for instance, it is the performance of a work that we appreciate, with all of its possible variations, more than we do the "original" script or notation (the work of Shakespeare being one of many notable exceptions, of course) (Goodman 112–115). During the Renaissance, considered to be a high point in the history of European art, painters learned their craft by spending years as apprentices, during which time they would imitate and copy existing paintings to build their skills; as one scholar put it, "Copying was the right and logical thing to do" during the Renaissance (Cole 31). We also might think of cover songs, like Jimi Hendrix's version of "All Along the Watchtower" or many of the songs performed on the television show *Glee* (2009–2015). One estimate is that there are about forty thousand songs with at least one cover version (Plasketes 1). With cover versions, we often derive pleasure from hearing a familiar song repeated but in a different style.

If we take it that all cultural texts connect to previous texts and are generally constructed through a process of repetition and variation, of borrowing and transforming, we still need to examine just *how* this process occurs and the different *forms* this process can take. We need to define and analyze some of the most prominent forms of intertextuality that appear within contemporary cinema culture. Intertextuality entails the specific, identifiable relationships that connect different texts to one another. There are many specific forms of intertextuality, including adaptations, series, sequels, trilogies, remakes, reboots, and franchises. We also encounter pastiche and parody, which are defined more by style than by narrative. It is helpful to clarify how these terms are used to describe certain categories of texts and textual relationships, so that we can see their complexities and understand some of the forces that help shape these categories. Indeed, all of these intertextual forms should be considered "cultural categories," meaning that the definition for each one is the product of a broad cultural process and discourse.

But we also need to acknowledge that the vast majority of those objects we call "adaptations," "remakes," "reboots," or "franchises," and so on are produced as commercial products designed to make money. As Kathleen Loock has asserted, cinematic forms like remakes, sequels, and spin-offs "are driven by commercial imperatives and rely on pretested material that they repeat, modify, and continue in order to ensure box-office success" (278–279). From this perspective, we cannot properly understand these different textual categories and intertextual relationships without acknowledging that these products are made as commercial endeavors. We must understand all of these categories as "industrial intertexts" that are produced, circulated, and consumed through a process of "industrial intertextuality." Within an analysis of the *Batman* franchise, Eileen Meehan coined a similar phrase, the "commercial intertext" (49, 58). Meehan uses this idea to describe how economic incentives drive the production of different texts with strong and identifiable intertextual relationships. As she states, "For most of American culture, corporate imperatives operate as the primary constraints shaping the narratives and iconography of the text as well as the manufacture and licensing of the intertextual materials" (49). However true this formulation is, it does not provide a means of understanding cultural texts as commercial products *and* as meaningful within popular culture more broadly.

I prefer, therefore, to use the phrase *industrial intertextuality* to describe how contemporary media texts connect with one another. "Industry" can and often does refer to the organized production of commercial products. But, as Raymond Williams importantly noted, "industry" can more generally refer to "work" (165). Thus, with the phrase "industrial intertextuality," we can also describe the work of amateurs and fans who produce adaptations and remakes of existing films, books, or television programs as fan fiction or fan vids, which typically do not get compensated with money (see Jenkins, *Textual Poachers*; Loock; Verevis). Indeed, in some notable cases, these fan productions gain a prominent place within popular culture and even get recognized and approved by commercial producers, critics, and mainstream media audiences. An example of this is *The Raiders of the Lost Ark: The Adaptation*, a shot-for-shot remake of *Raiders of the Lost Ark* (1981) that some teenagers made on Betamax and VHS over the course of the 1980s (Murphy). After copies of this remake circulated in an underground fashion, the filmmakers' efforts were covered in a story in *Vanity Fair* in 2004, and they were even able to meet with Steven Spielberg after he saw their work (Murphy). Ultimately, a documentary about the making of this fan remake was made in 2016, *Raiders! The Story of the Greatest Fan Film Ever Made* (2016), and gained distribution through Drafthouse Films and appeared on Netflix (Murphy).

However, fan productions on this scale or that gain this level of mainstream attention are relatively rare, especially when compared to the vast number of shorter fan vids that appear on YouTube or simply circulate among the makers' friends. But thinking of industrial intertextuality even more broadly, we can see that it permeates all of contemporary media culture, even when there is no identifiable text being produced. Indeed, this phrase can be used to describe the work that occurs in the minds of readers and viewers as they make the mental connections between the media texts they consume and the media they have consumed previously. When we see a movie based on a comic book that we have read, we inevitably connect the two texts in our minds, compare them, and assemble them in some relationship with each other conceptually. This mental activity is work, too. And finally, industrial intertextuality can be used to describe the work that it takes to make the various public, cultural discourses within which these texts get defined, described, analyzed, and critiqued. This might entail the paid work of movie and television critics, or it could be the activity of a group of friends discussing a film or television program with one another. Remakes and franchises are intertextual by industrial design, to be sure, but they accrue meaning through the broader work done to them when they circulate through culture.

One of the most common forms of intertextuality found in contemporary culture is the adaptation. Most commonly, this term has been used to describe films that take a narrative from an existing work of literature, like *Harry Potter and the Sorcerer's Stone* (2001). But as Linda Hutcheon writes, "If you think adaptation can be understood by using novels and films alone, you're wrong" (xi). Thus, more generally, adaptations can be understood as texts that take a narrative or some other fundamental element from a text produced in some other medium. Films based on novels are still adaptations in this account, but so are television programs based on comic books (*The Walking Dead*, 2010–), video games based on movies (*Alien vs. Predator: Extinction*, 2003), radio plays based on novels (Orson Welles's *The War of the Worlds*, 1938), and so on. Adaptations retell the story or transpose some crucial aspect of an existing text in another medium.

Because of this transposition across media, adaptations are not only intertextual but also intermedial. This means we must think about how different media relate to one another, which also requires us to think about the specific characteristics and capabilities of each respective medium through which a story gets told. As Robert Stam has noted, "each medium has its own specificity deriving from its respective materials of expression" (59). A considerable amount of criticism and scholarship related to adaptations has consequently debated what novels can do that films cannot, and vice versa (e.g., Chapman). In fact, many discussions evaluate how "faithful" or similar a film adaptation is to a novel and in this manner engage in what is called a discourse of "fidelity" (Stam 54–55). In these discussions, critics consistently align the quality of an adaptation with its fidelity to its source. A review in the *New York Times*, for instance, of *Sophie's Choice* (1982) evaluates both the film and the lead actress in terms of fidelity, stating, "In Alan J. Pakula's faithful screen adaptation of Mr. Styron's novel, Miss [Meryl] Streep accomplishes the near-impossible, presenting Sophie in believably human terms without losing the scale of Mr. Styron's invention" (Maslin). Similarly, a review of an early screening of *The Martian* (2015) on the fan website Ain't It Cool News stated, "I loved what I saw. It was an exciting, faithful adaptation of the book" (Copernicus). There are nearly as many of these kinds of discussions as there are adaptations.

Yet we must acknowledge that the transfer of a narrative from one medium to another is such a radical change that "fidelity" is never truly possible (Stam 55). Rather than evaluate an adaptation on the basis of its fidelity, Robert Stam proposes that we compare how each version tells a story differently, so as to better understand how stories are told and to better understand how a medium might impact the way stories are shaped (68–69). What was changed, and why might this be the case? What scenes were added or eliminated, extended or reduced, and did they appear in the same order? Broad questions like these are particularly helpful when we are thinking about adaptations beyond the scope of films based on novels. What does *Pirates of the Caribbean: The Curse of the Black Pearl* (2003) take from the theme-park ride of the same name, and how, and why? How is it important that I can "play" the character of Darth Vader in the video game *Star Wars Battlefront* (2015)?

In addition to such formal issues, it is vital to remember also that adaptations are a cultural category. Along these lines, Linda Hutcheon has referred to adaptations as "both a product and a process of creation and reception" (xiv), while Dudley Andrew has argued that we ought to approach adaptations sociologically (35). In this vein, we would do well not only to think about how stories change as they move from one medium to another but also to understand how both the stories and the medium function within culture more broadly, including to media makers and audiences. A substantial number of films, for instance, seek legitimacy and status by adapting respected works of literature; as Judith Buchanan notes, for instance, almost three hundred films were made based on plays by William Shakespeare between 1899 and 1927 (xvii). Given that all of these films were produced without dialogue, we can understand that for both their producers and audiences, these films had an appeal beyond fidelity to Shakespeare's scripts. Alternatively, we can understand the public and critical discourse around the fidelity of, for instance, *Sophie's Choice* or *The Martian* as expressing concerns over cultural status, legitimacy, and power as much as they engage with issues of artistic quality. With adaptations, in other words, we have to consider how each specific narrative gets defined and shaped by different groups and also the comparative social place and status that each medium holds.

In addition to adaptations, another significant type of intertextuality that occurs regularly, indeed repeatedly, within the cinema is the series. If adaptations largely tell the same story as has been told in an existing text in a different medium, then series largely appear as texts that tell different stories that share some basic component or elements within a single medium. Everywhere one looks, you can find series of books, comic books, and video games, and there have been film series for over one hundred years. (For example, the *Fantômas* series began in 1913; discussed in Gunning, "Intertextuality.") Jennifer Forrest defines series as "a group of films related by recurring core characters and in which each entry is an independent episode" (Introduction 3). But there remains some question about the "independence" of each member of a film series. True, some series tell stories about the same character as self-contained installments, such as most of the James Bond movies. Some series appear to have a chronology but are released out of chronological order, such as the *Indiana Jones* films. Others, such as *The Hunger Games* films or the *Twilight* movies, appeal to viewers specifically *because* each film follows a continuous plotline. Whereas adaptations generally repeat some element of an existing narrative, film series offer "something more." Sometimes this "more" is a new, independent story that features recurring characters and settings, and at other times "more" means continuing and extending an ongoing plotline.

But these last two examples, *The Hunger Games* and *Twilight*, point toward the complicated relationship between adaptations and film series, as each of these series of movies was based on a series of books. This practice of adapting a series across different media has occurred also for a very long time, such as with *The Amos 'n' Andy* radio program (1928–1960) being transferred to television (1951–1953) or the *Mission Impossible* films (1996, 2000, 2006, 2011, 2015), which adapt the television program of the same name (1966–1973). Further complicating this situation are cases where there are different series in different media that track the same character or story world, such as the comic book *Kanaan: The Last Padawan*, which tells the backstory of the character Kanaan, who also appears in the television program *Star Wars: Rebels* (2014–). There are also film series that adapt some elements of a series from another medium but then have their narratives diverge significantly, such as is the case with the *Bourne* films (2002, 2004, 2007, 2012, 2016). I mention all of these examples not to discredit the term "series" but rather to point toward the complexity and diverse array of texts that get placed in this category.

Two intertextual forms that relate strongly to series are sequels and trilogies. As Carolyn Jess-Cooke points out, sequels are an incredibly old intertextual form that can "be traced back to oral narratives dating as far back as Homer's *Illiad*" and that developed for many years as a "literary format" (2). Generally, the term "sequel" refers to any narrative text that continues the story of an existing text. The film industry most clearly indicates that something is a sequel when "Part 2" appears in the title, like

Jaws 2 (1978) or *Halloween 2* (1981). For scholars Forrest and Jess-Cooke, among others, this sense of narrative continuation is what separates the film sequel from the film series, as both assert that a series largely does *not* continue a narrative progressively forward (Forrest, Introduction 7; Jess-Cooke 5). By this logic, any sequence of films that had an ongoing story would count every film following the first as a sequel, no matter how many in number. It seems that it was in this sense that Manohla Dargis referred to *Star Wars: The Force Awakens* as a sequel, as noted in the introduction.

In fact, the term "series" gets used to describe these types of films as well, especially in cases when there are a large number of films within the same group. For instance, a news article about the fifth *Fast and Furious* film stated, "Over the last decade, Universal built the 'Fast' series with a singular focus on the underground car racing scene, and fans have consistently turned out," but then in the next passage, it stated that "the studio worried that another repetitive sequel wouldn't have the horsepower to draw new audiences" (Fritz). This single article points to a range of important issues. First, we see that the terms "series" and "sequel" can be used interchangeably by critics and still be understood by general readers. Second, this writer makes claims about "the industry" and even names the specific studio and thus points to the ways in which these terms and categories serve industrial purposes. And third, the article mentions fans and audiences and suggests that this group, on the one hand, wants a certain experience repeated and, on the other hand, wants that repeated experience to be novel in some important way. As a media scholar, I appreciate and often demand a precise use of language, so that we might best express our most sophisticated thoughts about a topic. But, as this article suggests, the categories and terms related to intertextuality are slippery, and it is perhaps exactly this slipperiness that allows for multiple groups of people to participate in the classification of these texts.

Like series and sequels, the term "trilogy" describes a grouping of multiple related texts. Yet trilogies are more rigorously defined and always consist of a group of three texts. Following this basic definition, though, trilogies appear nearly as complicated as series, sequels, and any other textual category. For instance, some trilogies are produced as such, as in the case of *The Three Colors* trilogy by Krzysztof Kieślowski, *Blue* (1993), *White* (1994), and *Red* (1994). Other trilogies, however, are understood as such by critics and audiences only after the fact or simply as the result of there being three films in a sequence, like *Rush Hour 1–3* (1998, 2001, 2007). Moreover, trilogies sometimes continue a single narrative across three films, such as with *The Godfather* films (1972, 1974, 1990), but other times are linked only by a common theme, such as with Gus Van Sant's "Death Trilogy" of *Gerry* (2002), *Elephant* (2003), and *Last Days* (2005). Whether linked by narrative or theme, as a production strategy or as a critical and audience category, film trilogies have the sequential nature of series and sequels but have a limit—until someone makes a fourth installment, confusing the entire situation yet again.

In the most general terms, film remakes are generally understood as films based on other films. Clear examples of this would include *The Fly* (1986), which is based on the earlier film of the same name (1958), or perhaps most notoriously, Gus Van Sant's *Psycho* (1998), which is an almost shot-for-shot remake of Alfred Hitchcock's film (1960). More recently, however, critics have noted the great number of television programs that remake earlier programs, leading one scholar to ask, "how . . . do we begin to discuss remaking practices that are becoming a significant feature of the television landscape" (Proctor, "Interrogating" 5)? Further, the term "remake" has also been used to describe video games that are based on previous video games. In light of this, we might more broadly and accurately say that remakes are intramedial intertexts. That is, if adaptations generally borrow a narrative from another text in a different medium, then remakes borrow a narrative from a text in the same medium.

A variant of the remake is the pastiche, a term that generally refers to texts that imitate the style of a previous text; these are texts that allude fairly directly to the qualities of another specific text or even an entire series or genre of texts. In the cinema, we can see a great number of the films of director Brian De Palma as pastiches, and he imitates, quotes, or alludes to films by Alfred Hitchcock in particular. Something like *Body Double* (1984), for instance, depicts a man witnessing an apparent assault of a woman in a nearby home through a telescope, which is the basic premise of the film *Rear Window* (1954). Moreover, a kissing scene in *Body Double* features a use of rear-projection and a spinning camera very similarly to a kiss scene in *Vertigo* (1958). The films of Quentin Tarantino are also full of quotes and allusions to existing films and genres, and one might consider them pastiches as well. *Inglourious Basterds* (2009), as just one example, takes and twists the title of the film *Inglorious Bastards* (1978). And although Tarantino's film does not truly repeat the narrative of the earlier movie, both films follow an unruly, brutal team of American soldiers as they fight Nazis during World War II; notably, this is also the premise for *The Dirty Dozen* (1967).

In these cases, we see that certain "auteur" directors have used pastiche as a device to quote and reference other films in a positive way. Similarly, some auteurs have referenced or recycled their own works as a means to further elaborate their artistic concerns, authorial sensibilities, and cultural status. Here, we might think of Richard Linklater's films *Before Sunset* (2004) and *Before Midnight* (2013), which follow up with the characters he first developed in *Before Sunrise* (1995). With this trilogy, Linklater followed a narrative across many years but, just as important, maintained and reaffirmed his directorial style through the dialogue and treatment of these characters. Somewhat similarly, we might think of Michael Haneke's remake of his film *Funny Games* (1997, 2007). In this case, the director reinforced his style and sensibility by making a shot-for-shot remake, the only differences being that the two films featured different performers and the original was in German and the remake in English. To this extent, these examples show how pastiche and other forms of cinematic recycling can be associated with a certain cultural status. However, some critics and scholars have derided pastiche quite intensely, such as Fredric Jameson, who asserts that pastiche and other kinds of overt cinematic intertextuality can be read as negative symptoms of "the postmodern condition" (16–20). Thus, the practice and the concept of pastiche, as with intertextuality more generally, has been used by different groups in a larger struggle for cultural meanings and legitimacy.

Film parody is a mode of cinematic intertextuality and remaking that, within the texts themselves, seeks to undermine or at least question the status of other specific texts or even genres and styles. That is to say, parodies *embody* a struggle over cultural status by spoofing existing texts and genres. Dan Harries defines parodies as those texts that emulate others so as to mock them, but he also acknowledges that parodies entail a process "that does indeed change and adapt to its cultural moment" (5–6). Thus, *Airplane!* (1980) parodies *Airport* (1970) and *Airport 1975* (1974), among other films and, truly, the entire cycle of disaster movies released through the 1960s and 1970s. Similarly, *Scary Movie* (2000) mocks a great number of contemporaneous horror movies, including *Scream* (1996), *The Blair Witch Project* (1999), and perhaps most directly, *I Know What You Did Last Summer* (1997). In all of these cases, the films parody specific films and genres that would have been recognizable to audiences at the time they were released, making these films relatively historically contingent. However, and as Harries points out, the comic devices used in film parodies, such as misdirection (62) or exaggeration (83), can make these films humorous even to audiences who are unaware of the specific source material being mocked (3). Finally, it is important to point out that although film parodies may be extremely popular with audiences, and some even get celebrated by critics, these films almost never earn awards or other signs of cultural prestige or status.

Remakes, pastiches, and parodies all repeat the narratives and styles of previous films and genres and regularly get caught up in larger cultural debates about quality, meaning, and legitimacy. Recently, the term "reboot" has also been used describe an increasing number of films that replicate some elements of previous films, but this term somehow dodges much of the baggage that comes with the term "remake." Yet, however much remakes and reboots appear similar, reboots have their own intertextual properties as well as their own cultural position and status, even if that status may be contested. Considering industrial and textual factors simultaneously, William Proctor has astutely defined the reboot specifically in relation to the remake. He writes, "a film remake is a singular text bound within a self-contained narrative schema; whereas a reboot attempts to forge a *series* of films . . . in other words, a remake is a reinterpretation of *one* film; a reboot 're-starts' a *series* of films that seek to disavow and render inert its predecessor's validity" ("Regeneration" 4). In this manner, movie reboots *do* remake an existing text, in the sense that reboots borrow elements from a film or set of films. But they do so in such a way as to generate subsequent films. In terms of narrative, then, reboots bring together (at least) two of the forms of intertextuality discussed earlier, namely, remakes (or adaptations within a single medium, often film) and series (or the extension of narratives, characters, and story worlds across a sequence of multiple texts). Reboots try to both remake and extend narratives at the same time. In this way, reboots bring together industrial pressures to create new productions, textual elements that can be "open" to further elaboration, and audience desires for novelty within a familiar frame.

In terms of textual properties and narrative design, reboots generally take a character or group of characters that already appear in a number of other cultural texts and present stories in which these characters and the story world are refreshed or redefined in some basic way. Many times, this involves a reboot going back to the "origins" of a character. A prime example here is *Batman Begins* (2005). Although the story of how and why Batman became Batman had been detailed in comic books decades earlier and although the 1989 *Batman* film, directed by Tim Burton, also offered a depiction of the character's origins, *Batman Begins* tells the story of how and why Bruce Wayne decided to dress up in a costume and fight criminals. Similarly, *Casino Royale* (2006) tells the story of how James Bond became "007," despite the existence of numerous films in which this was already the case. And *Man of Steel* (2013) is yet another example, as it retells the story of how Superman came to Earth and began to use his powers to defend the planet. A more complex case is the 2009 *Star Trek* film. Here, the narrative takes place before the events of the original 1960s television program. But the entire historical development of that story world changes when characters travel from the future and alter this "past." In this instance, all existing *Star Trek* programs, movies, and other texts remain "true" or valid, but this particular film, and the films that would follow, are able to rewrite the entire history of this story world, as it exists in a "parallel universe" of sorts.

Industrially, reboots are designed for copyright holders to reexploit an existing property but in such a way as to appear new, original, or novel enough that audiences will be interested in seeing this familiar property. An example along these lines is *The Incredible Hulk* (2008), which followed the film *Hulk* (2003) by only five years but was connected to the interlinked "Marvel Cinematic Universe" films like *Iron Man* (2008), *Thor* (2011), and *The Avengers* (2012). Further, as Chuck Tryon has pointed out, reboots can be made when an actor who has played a character has grown too old to do so any longer (434). More important, Tryon points out that some reboots are made so as to make use of new technologies, and he more specifically shows how *The Amazing Spider-Man* (2012) utilized 3-D technologies to reboot the earlier *Spider-Man* films (2002, 2004, 2007) directed by Sam Raimi (1–2).

Although reboots are industrially designed to generate a new sequence of films with recurring characters and story worlds, this chain of production depends greatly on whether a reboot is popular with audiences and makes sufficient money at the box office. Thus, we might see *RoboCop* (2014) as a "failed" reboot. Like many reboots, this film retold the origin story of the character from the 1987 film and altered many details of that story. Further, this film treated the second and third *RoboCop* films (1990, 1993) as though they did not happen. Most important, perhaps, critics referred to the 2014 film as a reboot even before it was released (for example, McIntyre; Hustad), and one of them even made it clear that "if 'RoboCop' is a hit, it could launch a franchise for MGM" (McIntyre). But the film received only a lukewarm response from critics and audiences, and more important, it was not a blockbuster financial success. This has led not to a sequel but rather to debate as to whether another film in this line will be made (Brew); perhaps this "reboot" will simply be rebooted.

As one critic noted in relation to *RoboCop*, reboots occur within the industrial and cultural context of media franchises. As Derek Johnson describes, media franchises have come to be understood as "a logic of multiplied cultural production," involving "networks of collaborative content production constituted across multiple industrial sites" (6). At the heart of media franchising, then, is a single intellectual property, owned and exploited by one company but also, through contractual agreements, exploited by other companies. These kinds of business arrangements have led to much of the intertextuality we see throughout contemporary culture. As a business logic and practice of textual production, media franchising aims for expansion. This expansion may take many forms, with franchises appearing across media and also as multiple versions of related products within the same media, such as with film series, television programs, spin-off films and programs, video games, comic books, toys, and so on. Think of the *Fast and the Furious* series, the films and television programs of "The Marvel Universe," or the various toys and movies based on *The Transformers*. Here, media corporations did not just produce texts and artifacts for commercial purposes but intentionally linked these texts into an intertextual web by design, creating a combined industrial/textual network.

Along these lines, Marsha Kinder has asserted, "by the 1980s this intertextuality and its commodification had been greatly elaborated and intensified" (40). For Kinder, this combination of intertextuality and commodified cultural production help to create what she calls a "supersystem of mass entertainment" (40). In a somewhat similar vein, Henry Jenkins has defined the contemporary links between media industries, texts, and audiences as "media convergence." Jenkins defines convergence as "the flow of content across multiple media platforms, the cooperation between multiple media industries, and the migratory behavior of media audiences who will go almost anywhere in search of the kinds of entertainment experiences they want" (*Convergence* 2). Whether you call it a "supersystem" or "convergence," it is clear that contemporary media culture is characterized by a high degree of industrially designed intertextuality, which links together numerous texts and consumer products, as well as media companies and audiences. Franchising is the business mechanism that supports this intertextuality and has become a term used by media-industry workers, critics, and general audiences alike to refer to a wide range of cultural texts and productions.

Yet the intertextual linkages among these texts and commercial products are not always the same, nor do they hold equal weight or importance for different groups of people. Jenkins has identified one of the more intricate intertextual relationships that can occur among some media franchises, which he calls "transmedia storytelling" (*Convergence* 20–21). Jenkins writes, "Transmedia story-telling is the art of world making. To fully experience any fictional world, consumers must assume the role of hunters and gatherers, chasing down bits of the story across media channels" (20–21). Put another way, transmedia stories bring together "multiple texts to create a narrative so large that it cannot be contained within a single medium" (95). Jenkins looks particularly at the way *The Matrix* story world was built through the strategic narrative linkages among three different films, a series of short animations, and a video game (95).

A more recent example would be a bundle of texts released by Disney that were designed to connect strategically with *Star Wars: The Force Awakens*. The comic book series *Journey to Star Wars: The Force Awakens—Shattered Empire*, for instance, picks up the *Star War* narrative where *Return of the Jedi* (1983) left off. Further, it features a young Poe Dameron, one of the heroes of the *Force Awakens* film. Similarly, the short story *Star Wars: The Perfect Weapon*, which was distributed to consumers as a digital file to be read on e-book readers and tablets, tells an adventure story about a character named Bazine Natal, who goes unnamed but appears in *The Force Awakens*. Finally, the video game *Star Wars Battlefront* allows players the ability to "play" through the Battle of Jakku, the results of which can be seen in *The Force Awakens*. In each case, these texts needed to stand on their own or to be enjoyable without connecting with the others but also to allow people who *did* engage with each text to see the connections among them and ideally to find that these connections added to their enjoyment of each one. Transmedia stories, then, can be thought of as a "series" that occurs across different media, where each text works independently and in concert with one another at the same time.

But most of the intertextuality that occurs within media franchising is not nearly so intricate or coordinated as this. Think, for instance, of the video game *Batman: Arkham Asylum* (2009). The game was produced by Eidos Interactive in collaboration with Warner Bros. Interactive Entertainment, an industrial linkage typical of franchises. Further, it used media-industry workers who had worked previously on *Batman: The Animated Series* (1992–1995), including writer Paul Dini and actor Mark Hamill, although the game had no overt connection to this cartoon. Rather, the "plot" for the game was developed as a "new" Batman story, not as an adaptation of an existing comic book or movie plotline. Nevertheless, the game represents Batman as a dark, grim figure that surely draws influence from the way in which the character appears in the Batman films directed by Christopher Nolan. And, indeed, it is difficult to imagine that this video game was not connected, in the minds of gamers, to the contemporaneous, immense popularity of *The Dark*

Knight (2008), which came out a year before the game. Multiple reviews of the game compared it to this film. One reviewer stated clearly, "Just as Christopher Nolan's 'The Dark Knight' introduced us to a grittier Batman flick on the big screen, Eidos Interactive and Warner Bros. Interactive Entertainment have partnered to deliver a darker and atmospheric adventure on the small screen in 'Batman: Arkham Asylum'" (Saltzman). This video game thus connects multiple industrial and textual elements of the Batman franchise but not in such a way as to alter or directly impact the narratives and representations occurring in other texts within the franchise.

In fact, an immense number of media franchise texts, and perhaps the majority of our encounters with media franchises, appear not in the form of texts, exactly, but rather as paratexts. Following the work of Gérard Genette, Jonathan Gray defines paratexts as those cultural products and materials that are adjacent to and strongly related to texts (6). Paratexts can include such materials as "opening credit sequences, trailers, toys, spinoff video games, prequels and sequels, podcasts, bonus materials, interviews, reviews, alternate reality games, spoilers, audience discussion, vids, posters or billboards, and promotional campaigns" (Gray 4). While each of these items might be taken on its own, as a text in its own right, the relation among them and to the supposedly "primary" text is paratextual. As Gray describes, paratexts shape our understandings about texts, even to such a degree that we may never encounter a "primary" text and yet still have a strong sense of it through our encounters with paratexts. You may have never seen a *Transformers* movie, but you likely have a good sense of what it is like. Moreover, you probably know that there are a huge number of Transformers toys and have a good idea about how they work, although you may have never played with one. Thinking about paratexts in this way helps us to see that texts are not "primary" or "central" at all within culture, as paratexts are all around us and significantly shape our engagement with texts and popular culture more generally. Considering the widespread proliferation of paratexts and considering that the great number of popular culture "texts" are, in fact, paratexts, we can gain a number of new understandings about how media culture is made and how we engage with it. All texts are paratextual, in the sense that they all refer to others, pointing to others and orienting our attitudes to other texts.

Indeed, this chapter began by indicating that *all* texts are connected to others; this is the very definition of the way we think of cultural "works" or products *as* texts. Yet a goal of this chapter has been to show that these connections among texts, this sense of intertextuality, require work. Media companies produce texts based on others, audiences work to link these textual experiences together, and critics and audiences debate about the nature, meaning, and importance of these connections. We may agree, then, with Roland Barthes that we ought to think of culture in terms of "texts" rather than "works," but then we should also think of all the "work" needed to produce, understand, and discuss the texts that constitute today's media culture.

2

UNDERSTANDING
FILM REMAKES

The *Oxford English Dictionary* defines the remake as "a remaking of a film or of a script, usually with the roles played by different actors; an adaptation of the theme of a film." Although there are some slippery terms here, like "adaptation" and "theme," this somewhat circular definition fits with many commonsense ideas about remakes. However, dictionary definitions often aim for generality at the same time that they seek clarity, and film remakes are actually quite complex. So, rather than simply taking the dictionary at its word, we might begin by looking at how and where film remakes get defined in the first place, by different groups and in different circumstances. Constantine Verevis has been especially helpful in this regard, as he has previously shown that remakes get defined through a broad cultural process that involves movie producers, critics, and audiences (2, 29). Remakes are more than a collection of texts with certain properties. They are also a crucial means of organizing and understanding media production and reception. Thinking about film remakes in this multidimensional way allows us to examine how remakes embody, express, and amplify struggles for meaning and power within our contemporary world.

Defining film remakes only helps us understand them to a certain degree, and understanding how they *get defined* similarly provides only some help when we try to understand and analyze specific examples of remakes. So, in addition to looking at some of the different contexts in which remakes have been defined, it is important to develop an analytical lens through which we might approach our encounters with film remakes. While it is tempting and actually quite logical to understand a film remake in relation to the specific film that it remakes, this kind of one-to-one comparative analysis offers only limited insights into what a remake meant to both filmmakers and contemporaneous audiences. Consequently, in addition to "looking back" to a single source for a remake, we should "look across" at other films and cultural texts that appeared around the same time as the remake. Looking across at this range of material helps us see the larger cultural context that influenced remakes, the people who made them, and the audiences who watched them. Like all movies, film remakes borrow from a wide array of sources, and looking at this broader range of intertextual connections can provide a more complex and accurate picture of film remakes and their importance within cinema culture.

The very word "remake" suggests *making* or producing something. This might lead us to think of remakes, at least initially, from the perspective of filmmakers and movie producers or, to put it another way, to examine remakes from an industrial perspective. When thinking about film remakes from an industrial point of view, we have to wonder why someone would make something anew and what allows him or her to do so in the first place. Like other forms of industrial intertextuality, film remakes raise the issues of intellectual property and copyright. And, in fact, the history of film remakes intersects with the history of copyright laws in notable ways. When cinema first appeared in the 1890s in the United States and in Europe, there were no copyright laws that clearly regulated film. Partly as a result of this, early filmmakers frequently copied one another's films. But here, at the very beginnings of the cinema and at the origins of the film remake, there is already a complex issue. Filmmakers in the 1890s and early 1900s copied other people's films in two distinct ways. First, they actually *physically copied* the film, in a process called "duping" that resembles what people now call movie "piracy." Second, they filmed a new movie that closely resembled the content of an existing film, which is what we commonly now understand as "remaking."

It wasn't until the early 1900s that copyright laws in the United States covered cinematic works and, in the process, defined the remake as a distinct category of film. In a case from 1905, *American Mutoscope and Biograph Co. v. Edison Manufacturing Co.*, the judge's ruling clarified the difference, legally, between film duplication (duping) and the refilming of similar staged scenes and events (remaking) (Forrest, "Personal" 93). Yet this case did *not* make unauthorized remaking illegal (95). That came about after another court case, which tied a film's copyright to an underlying *written* source, whether that was a novel, play, or screenplay, and provided the owners of that copyrighted work the exclusive right to profit from any adapted dramatizations of it, including film remakes (108). Although this particular court case was more focused on adaptations than on remakes, the ruling ultimately made a film's *narrative* protected by copyright. Therefore, film remakes got defined, legally, as films that told the same or very similar stories as a previous film. After the law was changed in 1912 to include cinema, one had to own the copyright to the previous film or else pay the owner for the right to produce a remake (Decherney 13)—unless, of course, one made an illegal remake, of which there are many examples. But the point here is that remakes got defined, legally and industrially, as films that told similar stories as previous films, and in order to make a remake, one generally needed the rights to this earlier film.

This industrial definition for film remakes has persisted through to today. Nevertheless, this understanding does not fully account for why filmmakers might create remakes and how they define remakes through the very process of production. As with all forms of industrial intertextuality, we might assume that remakes are simple attempts to cash in on a story or character that was already successful. And perhaps this is true in some cases, to some degree, such as with Peter Jackson's version of *King Kong* (2005), based on the film that was quite successful in the early 1930s. But in many other cases, remakes have come from films that did *not* gain widespread commercial success. An example here might be something like *Insomnia* (2002), based on the Norwegian film with the same title (1997). While the original film earned positive reviews from American film critics and although it made modest earnings in European theaters, it did not get widespread distribution in the United States or earn very much at the American box office. In this case, the original was a foreign film and had subtitles, and this fact no doubt contributed to its lack of commercial success in America. Nevertheless, this example disproves the notion that only successful films get remade.

Thus, we might think of remakes as attempts by film-makers and movie studios to take an earlier film and "get it right," whether that means improving on an earlier success or turning a former failure into a success for the first time. Thomas Leitch asserts in his masterful analysis of remakes that remakes make an implicit rhetorical promise to audiences to be "just like their originals only better" (45). What counts as "better" is always flexible, but this notion of remakes being "new and improved" versions of older films appears as a common motivation for many remake productions. Sometimes it is a matter of changing film technology, such as when Warner Bros. and other studios remade many of their own silent films as talking pictures following the invention of sync-sound film in the late 1920s. Or sometimes the "improvement" consists of the use of new stars and up-to-date cinematic style, such as with *Gone in 60 Seconds* (2000). And yet other times, a remake may try to adapt a literary text more "faithfully" than a previous version did, such as with John Carpenter's *The Thing* (1982), which follows the novella *Who Goes There?* much more closely than *The Thing from Another World* (1951). In all these cases, film producers treated remakes as creative and commercial opportunities, as springboards for new film production.

One of the more complex and sometimes problematic forms of "improvement" is what I have called the *transnational film remake,* or films made in one national or cultural context and then remade in another (Herbert, "Transnational" 5). *Insomnia,* mentioned earlier, is one case of this, but there have been hundreds of others made over the entire history of the cinema; some recent and notable examples include *The Ring* (2002), *Let Me In* (2010), and *The Girl with the Dragon Tattoo* (2011). Each of these films, and many more like them, are Hollywood remakes of foreign films. While the industrial and intertextual relationships between such films and the originals are intricate and profoundly complex, remakes like these largely demonstrate Hollywood's dominance within the global media market (Herbert, "*Sky's*" 31), as these films typically have greater production and marketing budgets and make significantly more money than the originals do—even in the national markets where the originals were made. Problematically as well, Hollywood remakes of foreign films typically abstract the stories and reduce the cultural specificities found in the originals; in other cases, Hollywood remakes foreign films that were already lacking in cultural specificity. Nevertheless, Hollywood is not the only industry that engages in this sort of remaking, and transnational remakes can be found all over the world and borrow from a wide array of cultural sources (Smith and Verevis 7–8), such as Turkish remakes of Hollywood films or Bollywood remakes of Korean films.

These alternative trajectories point toward the wide-spread practice of remaking as well as the ability of film-makers around the globe to adapt foreign films according to different cultural norms and cinematic conventions.

Remakes of all sorts indicate that filmmakers assume that there are new audiences for old material, as long as that material is refilmed and changes are inevitably made to the original in the process. Whatever the intentions of studios and filmmakers, however, they merely *hope* that there are these new audiences. But the ways in which audiences and critics actually react to remakes, and define film remakes through their reactions, can be quite com-plex and even differ from the ways in which remakes get defined through copyright and the production process. In fact, we might think of "remake" as having an even clearer, although highly contested, identity in the realm of film reception than in film production. Film remakes are reg-ularly disparaged in film criticism and fan discourses. In these instances, remakes are seen as unoriginal, inauthen-tic, crassly commercial, unnecessary, or otherwise lacking in some respect, and often these criticisms are founded on the very fact that the film is a remake.

Negative discussions of remakes are consistent throughout the history of commercial filmmaking in the United States. After studios began remaking silent mov-ies as talking pictures in the late 1920s and early 1930s, for example, many critics and film-industry publications criticized these remakes or noted their lack of popularity with audiences. A story from 1931 in the *Los Angeles Times* asserted, "remakes of ancient pictures, reproduced as talkers, in short, are found unpopular" (Kingsley). More pointedly, another story from the following year had the headline, "Tradition Trampled Upon as Films Revive Classics," and began with the assertion, "It's up again. The troublesome old question of whether to challenge tradition and remake the classics . . . or let sleeping dogs lie" (Scheuer). This story indicates how remakes were judged negatively *as remakes* and therefore points to the fact that originality was to be celebrated and that remakes, specifically, challenged ideas regarding cinematic originality and artistic quality. In fact, whereas critics and general movie viewers may express disappointment because a film *adaptation* did not follow the source novel close enough, many people criticize remakes, and the entire practice of remaking, because such films follow their sources too closely.

Other responses to remakes have been more balanced or ambivalent, however, both presently and historically. An article from 1937 asked, for instance, "Are re-makes of old films successful? This is today's most bitterly disputed question. . . . To date, it's a draw" (Miller). However, even this account, as with those cited earlier, evaluates the "success" of remakes in terms of both industrial objectives, or money, and artistic quality, as observed by other critics and general audiences. That is to say, even when remakes are evaluated in a "balanced" way, these evaluations also balance industrial and artistic concerns, as though the two were inseparable even as they may be opposed. Remakes have been defined in the critical discourse, then, as commercial products that always risk artistic failure because of their industrial identity *and* because of their lack of originality.

This general understanding of film remakes can be seen in any number of reviews of specific film remakes. In a review of *Freaky Friday* (2003), for example, the author states, "'Freaky Friday' shows how a remake should be done. Take a fondly remembered but imperfect movie, update it smartly without being too hip, stay away from winking references to the original, and cast charming and bright actresses" (Means). Although the remake of *Carrie* (2013) got a few positive reviews, at least as many were critical of the film. One reviewer wrote, "When you live in a popular culture predicated on sequels, remakes, rehashes, and clones, you grab what originality you can. For that reason, some of us were looking forward to 'Carrie,' a new version of the 1976 Brian De Palma classic. . . . I guess we had our hopes too high. The new 'Carrie' is a thoroughly dispiriting remake" (Burr). Although the review of *Freaky Friday* is positive and the review of *Carrie*

negative, both show how these individual films were evaluated in terms of a larger industrial tendency to produce
remakes and in terms of their artistic quality, specifically
in relation to the previous films that these films remade. It
seems that a remake succeeds or fails, critically, largely on
the basis of its intertextual status as a remake, a cinematic
category that is troubled from the start by its association
with the commercial interests of the film studios.

We can see this definition perhaps even more clearly
when writers use "remake" as an oppositional term. A
review of *Kiss of Death* (1995) stated that the film "is more
than just a remake of the famous 1947 film noir of that
name. It's a smart deconstruction and reconstruction that
throws more noir onscreen than this gangbusting thriller
had the first time around" (Carr). Here, the critic upholds
the idea that remakes are opportunities to improve on an
existing film. Just as important, this review praises the film
as being better than "just a remake," implying once again
that remakes are generally artistic failures. In what is perhaps an even more notable example, one critic asserted,
"Let's face it—'Mystery, Alaska,' is really just a remake of
'Rocky,' with ice hockey replacing boxing. And it's a pretty
good remake" ("Feel-Good"). Here, a critic has noticed
that an "original" film, in this case *Mystery Alaska* (1999),
has a very similar narrative as a previous film and calls it a
remake despite the fact that it is actually not (officially) a

remake of *Rocky* (1976). The critic appears to use the term "remake," then, both to indicate a film's lack of originality and then to point out what actually is new or innovative in the film. To this extent, this review reinforces the definition of remakes as films with similar stories that always risk artistic failure as a result of their lack of originality. Remakes, more than other kinds of films, apparently invite comparative evaluations and are generally understood by critics to be not as good as other films. Remakes have something to prove.

The truth is that filmmakers, film critics, and audiences also have something to prove in the way they approach and respond to film remakes. In each case, these different groups use remakes or define remakes in ways that support their own position within culture. Film remakes express struggles for cultural power, as do our discussions of these remakes. For movie studios, film remakes express industrial and cultural power to the extent that these films embody the studios' ability to capitalize and recapitalize on the intellectual properties that they own. For filmmakers, film remakes entail a struggle for legitimacy inasmuch as they allow filmmakers to pay homage to or improve on an earlier film. In this way, remakes allow filmmakers to demonstrate their love for cinema itself at the same time that they may express their own ingenuity and creativity. For critics and fans, remakes appear as opportunities to think about and comment on the commercial nature of mainstream filmmaking and to demand a certain degree of artistry, novelty, and inventiveness from movie studios and filmmakers. If remakes display the film industry's power to produce and reproduce movies with similar narratives, then remakes also give critics and fans occasions to demand something "more" from these same movie producers.

Nevertheless, in all these instances, these different groups largely define remakes in one similar way. Specifically, people generally define remakes in relation to a single film—by relating them and comparing them to the "original" film that is being remade. We might think of these kinds of comparisons as "looking back," as they look backward in time to the single "original" film and evaluate it in relation to a more recent remake. And, because an original film and a remake are separated by time and because these are different films to the extent that a remake is a *new* production (even if it copies various aspects of the earlier film), viewers will notice a great number of differences between the films as much as they might see similarities. To this extent, "looking back" seems to begin with formal or textual issues. That is to say, we generally notice and compare an original and a remake on the basis of their form and content. Even if we look to various explanations for how and why two films look different, such as the use of different filmmaking technologies or even the different historical and social contexts that may have influenced the content of the two films, many people still first approach remakes on the basis of their formal properties.

But what are the formal, textual aspects of the films that critics and audiences actually compare? Typically, we compare the narratives and styles of the two films. Film theorist Constantine Verevis has provided an incredibly helpful system for making narrative and formal comparisons among remakes. He asserts we should use a "semantic/syntactic" approach toward this analysis (84). That is, we should look at the individual elements that appear in a film, including characters, locations, and props (the semantic elements) as well as the overall plot structure and relationship among the different characters, locations, and objects in a film (the syntactical elements). Some remakes will keep an abundance of the same characters, including the same names, as well as locations, such as with *True Grit* (1969, 2010). Alternatively, some remakes will significantly change characters and setting, such as *A Fistful of Dollars* (1964), a western genre remake of the samurai film *Yojimbo* (1961) that kept the overall plot of the earlier film. In addition to narrative elements and structures, Verevis also indicates that we should attend to issues of film style (85). A number of remakes significantly change the style of the original, such as *Breathless* (1981), and these changes in style constitute much of the innovation or novelty of these kinds of remakes. Other films do not remake anything *but* the style of previous films, as in the case of *The Hateful Eight* (2015), a pastiche of 1960s-era, wide-screen western genre films. Many remakes mix and match these elements in such different ways that it would be impossible to account for all of the specific variations here. But it is important to note that remakes consistently invite comparisons of their stories and styles.

Although it is useful and illuminating to compare remakes in these ways—according to their narrative elements, narrative structures, and styles—there will still remain questions about *why* these changes occurred and what they meant to contemporaneous film producers and audiences. Even when we "look back," there are multiple issues that we should consider when trying to understand the similarities and differences between a film and its remake. Industrially, there may have been a change in film technologies that impacted the production of a remake. Perhaps a remake used color film, while the original was in black and white, or perhaps the remake was a sync-sound film and the original was silent. Also, most remakes use different actors and stars than the original films did, and in this way, these remakes inevitably

convey a different tone and sensibility based on the per-
formances and star images of the different performers.
Similarly, remakes are typically made by different directors than the original films were. As a result, these films
may exhibit different "personalities," or styles of film
authorship. And finally, from an industrial perspective,
an original film and a remake may have been made with
different rules of censorship in place. This might mean
that the original was made during the era of the "Production Code," when every film had to follow certain rules
self-imposed by the Hollywood studios in order to be
acceptable to a general audience, while the remake was
made after the MPAA ratings system was put in place in
1968, and different films might be for general audiences
(PG) or adults (R).

Factors like these only represent the historically changing industrial concerns. Original films and remakes are
separated equally by historically changing social and cultural contexts, which also greatly shape the production
and reception of remakes and all other kinds of films. In
order to examine film remakes in this light, one might
examine the narrative and style of the film in relation to
major themes and topics that recur in news stories from
around the same time as the release of the original film
and the remake. Of course, no commercial film that is
designed to entertain audiences, including remakes, will

reflect social reality in a direct way. But entertainment films *do* often incorporate, casually reference, or indirectly respond to social issues and concerns of their historical moment. Just as all films are "intertextual" and draw influence from all manner of previous films, cinema is also intertextual in relation to social discourses.

Thus, for example, we might note that *You've Got Mail* (1998) is a remake of *The Shop Around the Corner* (1940) that has the main characters interact anonymously via email rather than through written letters, as occurs in the original film. Here, the remake updates an existing plotline by incorporating a new technology, one that was becoming commonplace in the late 1990s; moreover, the very title of the film is the slogan for America Online, or AOL, which was a major internet and email provider at the time and which many moviegoers likely used. *You've Got Mail* is more than just a remake or an update, then, but also a commentary on the contemporaneous social milieu, which was being rapidly transformed by new technologies and the social interactions they facilitated.

This last point suggests that we might need to do more than simply compare a remake to the original film in order to fully understand why a remake looks and feels the way it does. In addition to "looking back" through history, we need to "look across" and examine film remakes in relation to other films, other elements of visual culture, and even other social discourses from around the time the remake was released. Indeed, it is often very helpful and revealing to look at a remake in relation to films released around the same time that have no clear connection to the remake, as well as television programs, video games, advertisements, and all sorts of other cultural texts. In this way, we can get a better sense of what the contemporaneous styles and idioms were that shaped the way a remake was made and understood by audiences.

A good example here might be *Clash of the Titans* (1981, 2010). Although both films retell a handful of Greek myths related to the hero Perseus, culminating with him fighting the Kraken, each movie aligns with the cinematic conventions of its respective historical moment. For instance, the 1981 film features a humorous, robotic owl that chirps and beeps as it helps the protagonist in his quests, recalling the narrative function and style of R2-D2 in *Star Wars* and *The Empire Strikes Back* (1980). The 2010 remake, on the other hand, draws from the grandiose style and imagery found in *The Lord of the Rings* trilogy of films earlier that decade (2001, 2002, 2003). Like those films, the remake of *Clash of the Titans* features the heavy use of computer-generated effects and sweeping virtual camera movements over large computer-enhanced landscapes. We would likely notice these and other formal and narrative details if we examined the remake only in relation to the earlier film. But without looking at other films and media from the era, we would lose a sense of how these narrative and stylistic elements "made sense" to contemporaneous producers and audiences and how each film reflected and reacted to larger tendencies within American cinema.

To further elaborate how film remakes can be understood formally, industrially, and culturally by both "looking back" and "looking across," it is productive to analyze a handful of specific cases. To begin, we can look back all the way to the very beginnings of cinema. We might assume that remakes are a relatively new phenomenon, that remakes are symptomatic of a contemporary obsession with cinematic recycling and cultural nostalgia. But this is simply not the case, as film remakes are as old as cinema itself. Following Thomas Edison's creation of the kinetoscope in the early 1890s and after the brothers Auguste and Louis Lumière first unveiled their cinématographe in 1895, these inventors and other early filmmakers remade both their own and others people's films. For instance, the Lumière brothers photographed multiple, extremely similar versions of a train pulling into a station. As scholars Martin Loiperdinger and Bernd Elzer have observed, "Three versions of *L'arrivée du train à La Ciotat* are known to have existed: Louis Lumière shot the first probably during his stay in La Ciotat between January 16 and February 3, 1896. . . . The third version is the famous and universally known *Arrival of the Train*. . . . Not until the summer of 1897, however, did Louis Lumière shoot this version" (103).

In what is probably the first version, a train comes to a stop at a station, moving from the right of the screen to the left at a diagonal to the camera. This version features a man in a light-shaded suit with a bowtie and a short beard, who comes off the train and looks directly at the camera; it also depicts a group of men in suits entering the frame from the right to board the train. The film identified by Loiperdinger and Elzer as the third version, on the other hand, differs notably as it begins with a man pushing a cart, who leaves the frame to the right, before the train pulls into the station (107). When the train pulls into the station, it does so at a very similar angle as in the earlier film; yet it differs also by depicting many women approaching the train to board it. Beyond these subtle differences, however, the films appear identical and were likely intended to do so.

Thomas Edison arguably made his own "version" of *Arrival of a Train* as *Black Diamond Express* (1896). This film takes place in a rural outdoor setting and depicts a train approaching the camera from the left of the screen. It then curves directly toward the camera before exiting the screen to the right, while a group of men stands next to the train tracks on the left. Although this film has obvious differences from *Arrival of a Train*, the primary visual attraction of *Black Diamond Express* remains the same: a train rushing toward a camera. Moreover, *Black Diamond Express* was itself remade a number of times following its release (Musser 96).

One might object to calling any of these single-shot, minute-long films "remakes." Although they depict similar imagery, these early films did not really convey a proper story or narrative. As Tom Gunning has asserted, such films constitute a "cinema of attractions," which were precisely the type of films that dominated in world cinema until around 1906 ("Cinema" 64). As Gunning describes, early cinema was not designed to tell stories at all, or at least not as their primary objective. Instead, early films presented viewers with scenes of visually interesting subjects. This might entail an image of a woman dancing or of cats in a staged boxing match or of a young child's first attempts at walking. Very few of these "attraction" films have much of a narrative but rather depict amusing vignettes. Thus, if we think of remakes as more than just a copying of a narrative, as copyright law eventually asserted, but rather as the reproduction of very similar scenes in a new cinematic production, then the *Arrival of a Train* films as well as *Black Diamond Express* certainly count. Moreover, by looking across as well as back, we can situate these films in relation to a greater aesthetic and industrial tendency within cinema culture more generally. Images of moving trains might not constitute a narrative, but such films and their remakes become much more understandable within the larger "cinema of attractions" context.

Perhaps unsurprisingly, remakes appeared just as important within the emerging narrative cinema of the first decade of the 1900s. As Gunning also notes, one of the first cinematic genres that developed and played with narrative form was the "chase film," a multishot film that generally depicted people or vehicles moving across the frame, into a new shot, in a chase of some kind ("Cinema" 68). One such film was *Personal* (1904), made by the American Mutoscope and Biograph film company. In this film, a man places an advertisement in a newspaper asking that an attractive woman meet him in front of Grant's Tomb. However, nearly ten women arrive looking to garner his affection. Overwhelmed, he flees the area, and the large group of women chases him through fields and woods, across a river, over a bridge, and so on. Eventually he stumbles, and the fastest of the women appears at his side. He appears to propose to her and holds her arm as the rest of the women arrive, and the new couple brushes them off and wanders away. Although the "plot" of this film is relatively weak, it does feature a central protagonist, an initiating problem or incident that leads to a series of complications, and a final resolution, all of which gets depicted in a series of shots that are linked by continuity edits.

This exact scenario and manner of representation was duplicated in another film from the same year, called *How a French Nobleman Got a Wife through the New York Herald "Personal" Columns*, made by Edwin S. Porter at the Edison film company. Although this remake is a few minutes longer that the earlier film and although it features some imagery not found in the source film, it relies on the same premise, even beginning at Grant's Tomb, and largely repeats the same venues for the chase, such as when the group crosses over a bridge and then a fence. This film, then, not only was a remake of *Personal* but also shows how the practice of remaking was intertwined with the development of cinematic storytelling techniques. These two films were so similar, in fact, that it led to a copyright infringement lawsuit, discussed earlier, through which the dupe and the remake were legally distinguished (Forrest, "Personal" 93). Although the judge in this case ruled that the second film was different enough that it did not constitute an illegal "imitation" (Decherney 66), these films do reflect the increasing importance of narrative within the cinema of the time and the ways in which remakes were linked to narrative similarities between films.

Once cinema was clearly established as a narrative art in the 1910s, remakes were more like we understand them today—films based on previous films or films with very similar stories as earlier films. But even during this time, there was much experimentation and development in the formal and stylistic devices through which narratives were delivered. In some cases, in fact, film remakes were important to these changes, as they allowed filmmakers to innovate on existing premises. An example of this can be seen with Pathé Frères's *The Physician of the Castle* (1908; aka *A Narrow Escape*) and D. W. Griffith's remake of this film, *A Lonely Villa* (1909). Both films tell the story of a doctor who is called away from his home and family by bandits on a fictitious medical call. Once the doctor is away, the bandits invade the home, and the remaining family members barricade themselves within the house, moving ever deeper as the bandits progress further. Eventually, the wife manages to call the doctor and alerts him to the threat. The doctor races back to his home and, with the aid of police, subdues the bandits just as they reach the family, saving them in a last-minute rescue.

Many differences between these two films appear superficial, but others are more significant. For example, the geography within the home in *A Narrow Escape* is somewhat vague, whereas *A Lonely Villa* maintains a more consistent arrangement of space, with the family retreating from room to room exclusively to the right of the frame. Perhaps most importantly, *A Lonely Villa* extends and elaborates the editing found in *A Narrow Escape*, which cuts between different scenes to suggest that they are happening simultaneously (Abel 194). As Tom Gunning has described, "Whereas parallel editing makes a dramatic appearance in the early Pathé film, it is limited to a sequence of ten shots. In Griffith's film, parallel editing functions throughout the film, involving more articulation within sequences. *The Lonely Villa* contains fifty-two shots compared to thirty for *A Narrow Escape*" (*D. W. Griffith* 204).

The more intricate editing of *A Lonely Villa* provides the remake with an increased level of suspense by better representing the different spaces in different shots. Indeed, all of Griffith's additions to this narrative serve to increase suspense and impending danger. Unlike *A Narrow Escape*, for instance, the Griffith film shows one of the bandits cut the telephone line by which the wife and the doctor communicate, making the danger she faces much more immediate. Likewise, the Griffith film has the doctor's automobile break down, causing him to be delayed as he solicits the aid of someone with a horse and carriage, which they eventually use in the race to the home. Thus, in this case, a remake has mimicked the story of a previous film but intensified its dramatic effects through a more complicated use of film form and style. We might even say, as some scholars have argued, that this remake embodies the development of narrative film style itself, which was a much-larger process occurring in the 1910s.

As cinema became more of a narrative art form, film producers drew from a wide array of sources for story ideas and plotlines. Many films adapted works of literature, and in turn, there were many "readaptations" of literary works, or remakes of films that were themselves based on an existing book. As just one example, we can look at some of the adaptations and remakes of *The Strange Case of Dr. Jekyll and Mr. Hyde*, by Robert Louis Stevenson, in order to see how different industrial conditions impacted the look and feel of each of the different films. This novella was published in 1886 and tells the story of a man, Dr. Henry Jekyll, who creates a potion that allows him to transform into a purely evil version of himself. This persona takes on the identity of Mr. Hyde and engages in various nefarious activities, most of which are unspecified within the book. Eventually, the Hyde personality becomes too powerful and takes over, leading Jekyll to commit suicide. The narrative is largely told from the perspective of an acquaintance of Jekyll's, a lawyer named Gabriel John Utterson. Utterson unravels this mystery through a series of encounters with both Hyde and Jekyll and, more importantly, by reading a letter from a friend of

Jekyll's who has seen him transform and, finally, by read-ing Jekyll's written confession about his experiments and descent into madness, which Utterson discovers at the very end of the novella.

The book was adapted into a silent film in 1920, directed by John Robertson and starring John Barrymore. This adaptation centers on Jekyll, who discusses (via inter-titles) his belief that human beings have both good and evil within them and who performs experiments to isolate those elements. Although Jekyll is engaged to be married, he begins carousing with women at bars and opium dens after he takes the potion that transforms him into Hyde. Eventually, the father of Jekyll's fiancée confronts him, and Jekyll transforms into Hyde and murders him. When his fiancée also tries to confront him, Hyde drinks poison and dies before he can harm her; she finds him, as Jekyll, dead, and the film ends.

Another version of this story was produced in 1920, starring Sheldon Lewis, making it impossible to call either of these adaptations "originals" or "remakes." More important to this analysis, however, is a sync-sound ver-sion from 1931, directed by Rouben Mamoulian and star-ring Fredric March, Miriam Hopkins, and Rose Hobart. Although this film merely credits the novel and not the 1920 film, it appears as a remake to the extent that it shares many aspects found in the earlier film that are distinctly not part of the novel. (Some of these elements do occur, however, in a theatrical adaptation of the novel from 1887). As with the 1920 John Barrymore version, for instance, the 1931 *Dr. Jekyll & Mr. Hyde* details how the character attends nightclubs after taking the potion that transforms him into Mr. Hyde. This film is even more explicit about his escapades, in fact, as it details how Hyde takes up with a nightclub singer named Ivy, and he actually abuses her and keeps her prisoner within an apartment that he visits when he desires. In one notable scene early in the film, he meets Ivy as Dr. Jekyll and saves her from being beaten by a man in the street; she then invites him into her apartment. As she complains of her injuries, she presses his hand between her thighs and then, in an extended shot, removes her garters and stockings and tosses them at him. Although Jekyll resists her flirting for the time being and will return to her later as Hyde, the scene is relatively candid in its representation of a woman revealing her body in her attempts to seduce a man.

This particular scene merits discussion because a very similar scene occurs in the 1941 version of the film, starring Spencer Tracy, Ingrid Bergman, and Lana Turner, despite the fact that this film credits only the novel and none of the film versions. As in the 1931 film, here we find Jekyll engaged to a young lady. After a dinner with her and her family, where he openly declares his belief in the two sides of the human personality, he rescues a young barmaid and takes her home. Just as in the earlier film, the woman complains of her injuries and flirts heavily with him. The arrangement of the bed and other props, the camera angles, and the lighting all resemble the earlier film. The barmaid even entices Jekyll by saying, "My ankle, don't you think you should look at that?" and there is a brief shot of her removing her garter and stocking. In addition to this conspicuously similar scene, the entire film plays out a similar drama to the previous two discussed here: Jekyll loses control of himself, and Hyde takes over; his fiancée becomes endangered by Hyde; he eventually commits suicide to save her.

What are we to make of this sequence of films, and what are we to make of the two similar scenes in the 1931 and 1941 versions? If we "look across" as well as "look back," then we will gain a much-better understanding of why they appear the way they do. First, we might begin with the 1920 version. Although a number of other creepy, macabre films were made that year, particularly several expressionist films from Germany like *The Cabinet of Dr. Caligari* and *The Golem: How He Came into the World*, we might better locate the 1920 *Jekyll and Hyde* within a larger tendency on the part of American filmmakers to produce "prestigious" literary and theatrical adaptations during this period. Thus, we also find that two of the biggest films from 1919 were *The Miracle Man* and *Broken Blossoms,* both based on pieces of literature, and in 1920, *Way Down East* and *Pollyanna* were big hits, the former based on a play and the latter on a novel. While all these novels, plays, and films differ from one another in narrative content, they all demonstrate Hollywood's burgeoning appetite for adapting literary and theatrical properties, in part because these sources had ready-made narratives and also because of the cultural status these works had already achieved.

The 1920 *Jekyll and Hyde* was also known for the performance of its star, John Barrymore, and we should see this film as well as the 1931 and 1941 versions of the film as "star" vehicles, capitalizing on the central conceit of the novel and requiring an actor to display his performance of two distinct personalities. Additionally, we should connect the 1931 version of *Jekyll and Hyde* to the larger cycle of monster movies of the early 1930s, which themselves were based on literary works published decades earlier, including *Dracula* (1931) and *Frankenstein* (1931). These were followed by such films as *The Mummy* (1932) and *The Invisible Man* (1933) and were preceded by the gothic features *The Hunchback of Notre Dame* (1923) and *The Phantom of the Opera* (1925). This last film presents a particularly important precedent, as the 1931 *Jekyll and Hyde* featured remarkable makeup effects for Jekyll's transformation into Hyde that many reviewers remarked on, as was the case with *The Phantom of the Opera*. Finally, we might connect this film to another gothic mystery film from 1930, *The Bat Whispers*, which was itself a remake of a silent film from 1926 that was adapted from a very successful stage play. While none of these movies are *directly* linked to the 1931 version of *Dr. Jekyll and Mr. Hyde*, they do present an overall generic context within which the film was made and viewed by audiences at the time.

And finally, we can understand the 1941 version not only as a star vehicle designed to showcase the acting abilities of Spencer Tracy and Ingrid Bergman, who was still relatively new to Hollywood, but also in terms of the changing industrial context of Hollywood. Although the later film mimics the bedroom/flirtation scene found in the 1931 film, it refrains from the overt display of sexuality found in the earlier version. This slight but significant alteration results, no doubt, from the imposition of the Motion Picture Production Code by the Hollywood studios in the time between when these two films were made. The "Code" or the "Hays Code," as it was called, laid out a set of rules for film studios about what could and could not be represented in movies in order to conform to a certain sense of middle-class morals and respectability. Many of these rules dealt with the representation of sex, sexuality, and gender. So, although there was a version of this code in effect when the 1931 version was made, this film is considered to be a "pre-Code" film and was able to be more overt because the code was not enforced with the rigor that it was from 1934 onward. After that, films had to be submitted to a board for approval before they could be released in theaters. This was the case for the 1941 version, and we can understand the alterations to the bedroom scene to be a consequence of this new institutional situation. Although audiences of the 1941 version likely "got it" and understood the implications of the flirtations in this scene, this film and others like it in the era were characteristically indirect in their suggestions about sex and sexuality. The film is clearly a remake, but without an understanding of the larger industrial context of 1941, we simply would not understand why this film makes the alterations it does.

Of course, by pointing out this industrial context and by connecting the 1920 and 1931 versions of *Dr. Jekyll and Mr. Hyde* to other literary adaptations or horror movies, we are only scratching the surface of the larger intertextual web and cultural context that impacted the production and reception of each of these films. Moreover, this brief analysis has not traced out the ways in which the *Jekyll and Hyde* narrative spiraled even farther outward and helped create a generic template and cultural myth of its own, which we can see in such examples as the parody *Dr. Pyckle and Mr. Pride* (1925), the sequel *The Son of Dr. Jekyll* (1951), a modernized television version from 1999, and even such reimaginings as the Incredible Hulk character from comic books, cartoons, and movies. All these films, and these specific remakes, are connected with innumerable other texts that shape them and get shaped by them in the wide network of texts we call "popular culture." We can and should look back and look across in order to better situate remakes within this web. Indeed, film remakes can help orient us as we try to understand the many forces that shape our culture, just as remakes help orient the production and reception of so many films.

3

THE EXPANSIVE AND INCLUSIVE
LOGIC OF FRANCHISES

At the 2014 Comic-Con in San Diego, the media company Legendary Entertainment announced the production of a new film about King Kong. This was reported to be a "surprise" to people in the audience because this was the first public announcement of the movie (Deadline Team). But it really wasn't very surprising that another version of *King Kong* was being made. After the giant ape first appeared in the titular film in 1933, in which he battled dinosaurs on a primeval island, fell in love with a movie actress, and fought airplanes and died atop the Empire State Building, the character appeared in many subsequent cultural texts. A sequel to *King Kong* was released later in 1933, in fact. Perhaps more interestingly, the Japanese film company Toho licensed the character from RKO and made a "mashup" film in 1962, in which King Kong battled Godzilla. Following that film, the Japanese animation company Toei licensed the character and made the animated series *The King Kong Show*, which played on US television for several years in the late 1960s. In the cartoon, Kong appeared as a dim-witted but benevolent figure that assisted a family that lived on his home of Skull Island.

In 1976, an "official" remake of *King Kong* was made. Although this film maintained much of the original film's narrative, the remake updated and adapted the text to new historical and industrial circumstances. For one, the main characters voyage to Skull Island not to make a movie, as they had in the 1933 film, but rather as part of an expedition to discover new oil reserves, a plot point that was likely inspired by the oil crisis in the earlier part of the 1970s. Further, the film depicts Kong climbing the Twin Towers of the World Trade Center and not the Empire State Building, thus capitalizing on the novelty of these structures, which had been built in 1973. The film also gestured toward the environmental consciousness of the era by featuring characters that were sympathetic to Kong, including a hippie-ish paleontologist played by Jeff Bridges. Kong was so misunderstood and sympathetic, in fact, that when he falls in love with the actress character, she appears to have an affection for the ape as well, as they share a tender interaction together on Skull Island and she cries in despair as he is attacked on the towers.

Another remake, directed by Peter Jackson in 2005, updated the film yet again by using the latest cinematic technologies. Whereas in the 1933 film the ape was made through stop-motion animation, and the 1976 Kong was actually a human in a gorilla costume, the 2005 film constructed the ape through digital animation and the use of motion-capture technology. Here, the movements and expressions of actor Andy Serkis were recorded as three-dimensional information within a virtual, digital space and animated in the form of a giant ape. Jackson and Serkis had famously used this technology a few years earlier to create the Gollum character in the *Lord of the Rings* trilogy; to this extent, this version of *King Kong* merely extended an established stylistic and technological trend.

This brief sketch of King Kong's intertextual existence shows that the character has appeared in a number of different narrative, industrial, and cultural contexts across time and that *Kong* has been remade in ways that conform to the cultural and industrial circumstances of different moments. So we should not be surprised by a new version of *King Kong*, which was released as *Kong: Skull Island* in spring 2017. What is striking, however, is exactly how this newest version updated the character for current commercial and cultural expectations. As a story from *Deadline Hollywood* indicated, Warner Bros. intended from the start to link this new version of King Kong to the company's remake of *Godzilla* from 2014 (Fleming). The story quoted a press release as stating, "[the production company] Legendary acquired rights to additional classic characters from Toho's Godzilla universe, including Rodan, Mothra, and King Ghidorah. This paved the way for developing a franchise centered around [the fictional organization] Monarch and anchored by Godzilla, King Kong, and other famous creatures" (Fleming). And indeed the company Monarch plays an important role in the film, and in a scene following the film's credits, we watch as the protagonists are shown drawings of Godzilla and the other monsters, indicating that the story is not over. Thus, whereas the character King Kong had appeared in a large number of texts over the course of many years, now a major Hollywood studio created a new text with the character that was *intentionally* linked to others and designed to lead to the production of even more texts and presumably toys and other merchandise as well. If King Kong had previously had been subject to sequels, remakes, and reinterpretations, now the character is part of a franchise of texts and products, all of which will have a "shared world," or a common fictional universe in which different characters and events will appear.

Media franchises entail the exploitation of an intellectual property across multiple cultural texts and consumer products, from movies and video games to backpacks and toy jewelry. Franchises are cultural texts whose intertextual linkages have been made by industrial design, with the aim to expand and spread that same property as far and wide as possible. With regard to film remakes, we have seen that it is important to "look back" to earlier films as well as to "look across" at contemporaneous films and cultural texts in order to understand why remakes look and sound the way they do. Media franchises take this interpretive approach and actually make it *part* of the industrial and cultural design of a film or television program. That is, franchises intentionally construct the web of connected texts that creates the "across" that we might otherwise examine. As examples, one can readily point to the *Twilight* books and films, the many versions of *Law & Order* that appeared on television in the 1990s and 2000s, and the "Marvel Cinematic Universe," which depicts the same pool of characters and story world in numerous films, television programs, books, video games, comic books, toys, and on and on. It seems as though franchises now appear everywhere and that franchising constitutes a major, if not the dominant, business logic currently driving the major Hollywood studios.

We need to look pointedly at the industrial and textual properties of media franchises in order to understand the complexity and significance of this cultural form.

Accordingly, this chapter surveys the historical development of media franchises and their contemporary industrial and intertextual logics, and it examines several specific case studies that illustrate how franchises can address issues of social diversity. Indeed, it is important to note that film and media franchises consistently address multiple social groups and occasionally incorporate issues of social difference as part of their endeavor to gain new audiences and spread an intellectual property as widely as possible. That is, franchises can be remarkably *inclusive* at the same time that they aim for commercial expansion. Derek Johnson has noted this tendency previously, focusing particularly on franchise "spin-offs" that aim specifically to appeal to female viewers and consumers (56–61). In addition to gender, we can see many cases where franchises engage with issues of race, ethnicity, and generation, among other categories of social difference. To my mind, these cases of "enfranchisement" of different social groups within the commercial logic of franchises and intellectual property signify some of the most complex and contradictory aspects of contemporary popular culture.

Clearly, there is nothing new about intertextuality, as all cultural texts connect to others; film remakes have been around since the invention of cinema, for instance. We should remain aware that adaptations, remakes, reboots, and the like are products of "industrial intertextuality."

Industrial intertexts are intentionally based on some previous text; they are typically designed to make money
in commercial markets; and viewers, audiences, and
fans help create and sustain the links among these texts
by consuming them, mentally connecting them, and
debating their qualities and discussing the relationships
among them. Film and media franchises, however, extend
and intensify the commercial aspects of this logic to the
degree that one simply must examine them as both industrial *and* intertextual objects simultaneously if we are to
properly understand their role in popular culture. With
franchises, we may have to return to Eileen Meehan's idea
of the "commercial intertext" even more than the idea of
the "industrial intertext," as the very *linkages* within a franchise are part of a larger commercial endeavor (49, 58).

As a cultural form, film franchises are fairly new. Avi
Santo has demonstrated that contemporary media franchises have their beginnings, or "generative precursors,"
in the early twentieth century, with companies that
licensed characters across different media (9). Nevertheless, Derek Johnson has shown that it is a relatively
recent phenomenon to think of cultural production in
terms of "franchises." As a way of thinking about media,
"franchising" developed significantly in the 1980s, until it
has become quite commonplace today (Johnson 6). As
a practice within the media industries, franchising was

borrowed from retail businesses, such as McDonald's, which had developed the franchise model in the 1950s and 1960s (Johnson 21, 33–41).

However, there are significant differences in the way franchising works in retail and in the media industry. Johnson writes, "While retail franchising uses contractual relations to emulate vertical integration across production, distribution, and sales, media franchising pursues horizontally multiplied production of media related through some shared, familiar content" (41). So in retail, for example, one could become a McDonald's franchisee and open up a new restaurant location, paying to do so through a license and then having access to the larger company's production capabilities and distribution networks. In media, franchising would mean that some company, like a video game company, pays a movie studio a license so as to have the right to make a video game based on an existing film. So, in addition to thinking of franchises as a set of texts and products, we can also think of *franchising* as a process, which requires the coordination (and occasional competition) among multiple production communities in the sharing and exchange of intellectual properties and other creative resources (Johnson 16–17, 22).

Think of *Harry Potter*. This series of books, the first of which appeared in 1997, was initially published by

Bloomsbury in the United Kingdom, but the company Scholastic paid for the rights to publish the book in the United States. The movies based on this series of books were made by Warner Bros. after the studio paid for the right to do so. Similarly, one of the video games based on these books and movies, *Quidditch World Cup*, was developed by the game company Magic Pockets, published by the video game giant Electronic Arts, and distributed by Warner Bros. Interactive Entertainment. There were versions of the game for multiple devices and platforms, including the Nintendo GameCube and Microsoft's Xbox. A theme park based on the Harry Potter characters and story world, called The Wizarding World of Harry Potter, opened in 2010 at the Universal Orlando Resort in Florida, which is owned by NBC-Universal. As just one last example within the seemingly endless chain of Potter-related texts and products, one can buy a Harry Potter necktie from the Noble Collection on Amazon.com for around thirty-five dollars.

All of these texts and products derive from a single intellectual property. Together, they form a network, an intertextual web of "Harry Potter." And all of these examples show that it took the work and cooperation of multiple companies to create and spread this franchise, as the rights to "Harry Potter" had to be transferred among them all, temporarily, contingently, and for a cost, in order for all these products to get made. Although no single person could acquire, consume, or even be aware of all the texts and products related to Harry Potter, each of us has encountered some subset of these texts and, in our minds and in our conversations with other people, built up our own world of "Harry Potter." Here is a network of texts, interwoven with one another and connecting multiple companies and an immense number of everyday people.

But we need to do more than just map out the chain of texts and products that constitute a particular franchise in order to see how franchises work and why they matter so much. So, in order to enter more deeply into the logic of film and media franchises, we can look to *Daniel Tiger's Neighborhood*. This children's program is produced for the Public Broadcasting Service, or PBS, which operates as a nonprofit television broadcaster and distributor. PBS has typically focused on programs with educational or cultural value, and the organization is particularly known for releasing children's programs, such as *Sesame Street* (1969–). It may seem strange or wrongheaded to begin with such an example, as franchises are more typically understood as commercial enterprises with dubious cultural or educational value. It may also seem odd to look to television for an illustrative example, considering that so many franchises appear to be centered on Hollywood blockbuster films. Yet it is precisely by looking at Daniel Tiger that we can see how the logic of industrial inter-textuality pervades all manner of contemporary media culture, with franchises moving across all sorts of texts, screens, and everyday products and objects.

Daniel Tiger's Neighborhood first went on the air in the fall of 2012, but news stories announced the program in 2011 and outlined some of the producer's larger goals. In some ways, this show sounded like a sequel, as one arti-cle noted: "*Daniel Tiger's Neighborhood* is based on the next generation of the original *Mister Rogers' Neighbor-hood* characters" ("PBS Announces"). And indeed, the show takes characters found in the earlier, long-running children's program but makes these characters older and in fact centers on their children; for example, the main character, Daniel Tiger, is actually the son of the orig-inal Daniel Tiger, who appeared on *Mr. Rogers' Neigh-borhood*. Further, *Daniel Tiger's Neighborhood* updates the earlier show by taking place exclusively within the Land of Make Believe, which was just one feature of *Mr. Rogers' Neighborhood*.

But the new show was also something of a remake. Whereas the Land of Make Believe in *Mister Rogers' Neighborhood* was represented with a toy trolley and min-iature houses and other structures, and puppets were used for the characters within it, *Daniel Tiger's Neighborhood* is an animated cartoon. The introductory song from the original show, "Won't you be my neighbor . . ." also opens the new program, with a new verse added to clarify that the program takes place in the Land of Make Believe. And like *Mr. Roger's Neighborhood,* each episode of the new show centers on some life lesson, such as cleaning up after playing or expressing frustration in appropriate ways. But whereas in the original show Mr. Rogers would address children viewers directly and talk them through the lesson to be learned from some incident or interaction, *Daniel Tiger's Neighborhood* dramatizes these lessons by showing Daniel or one of his friends encountering some difficulty and having parents or friends give advice about how to respond or behave. There are also musical refrains that clarify each particular lesson and that get repeated throughout an episode, such as "You've got to look a little closer to find out what you want to know" or "When you feel so mad that you want to roar, take a deep breath . . . and count to four."

This same news article indicated that *Daniel Tiger's Neighborhood* would obey a franchising logic, with the show merely serving as one aspect of an orchestrated intertextual network. It stated that the show was "a new animated multi-platform series" and that it "joins the PBS KIDS line-up of cross-platform content for kids ages 2 to 8. . . . With a transmedia approach, PBS KIDS is increasingly serving children wherever they live, learn, and play—on TV, online, through mobile devices, in the classroom, and through a new line of educational toys" ("PBS Announces"). However benign or even noble the stated educational goals are here, one immediately notes how this article situates Daniel Tiger within an intertextual system that spans across texts, media, and products. And while the company that produced the original *Mr. Rogers' Neighborhood*, the Fred Rogers Company, maintained its hold over the underlying intellectual property and was responsible for the production of the new show, this news story indicated the involvement of another media company as well, Out of the Blue Enterprises. Before working on *Daniel Tiger*, the people behind Out of the Blue had previously produced *Blue's Clues*, an immensely popular children's program that aired during the 1990s and early 2000s. Although *Blue's Clues* was also an educational program, it was developed for and aired on the commercial cable channel Nickelodeon. Perhaps indicating Nickelodeon's larger commercial interests, *Blue's Clues* was franchised across a number of different texts, media, and products, including books, toys, and a theatrical stage show.

Similarly, Daniel Tiger and his story world now appear in a wide range of popular media commodities, constituting a media franchise. But, as with the example of Harry

Potter described earlier, one might wonder which of these texts is central within this intertextual web or how kids (or their purchasing parents) might enter or navigate this network. A Daniel Tiger "spin-off" book, written by Becky Friedman and published by Simon and Schuster, provides an introduction to this character, his friends, and his world. In doing so, this slim picture book actually serves as an entryway into the franchise and, in fact, helps us understand some of the broader logics of media franchises. Titled *Welcome to the Neighborhood!*, the book begins with Daniel and his friend Prince Wednesday being told by King Friday that a "special visitor" has come to the neighborhood. The two kids then begin planning a party for this unknown visitor and travel first to a music shop to ask Music Man Stan to play some music at the party. To get there, the boys ride Trolley, and readers are shown a double-page map of the entire Land of Make Believe, orienting readers to the geography of the place. Once inside the music shop, Daniel and Wednesday also encounter Stan's daughter, Miss Elaina, and the three kids jump in excitement and pretend that they are rock stars; this particular segment introduces readers to a common feature of the television program, namely, that Daniel and his friends regularly slip into imaginary scenarios, with the décor, sound, and music changing around them to reflect their imaginings.

From there, all three kids go to visit Baker Aker and ask him if he could make "dinosaur bread" for the "Welcome-to-the-Neighborhood" party. Daniel then imagines what it would be like if the visitor was a dinosaur, and readers see a picture of Daniel actually seeing a small, blue dinosaur with a cartoony, friendly face. Daniel, Wednesday, Elaina, and O the Owl (who joined them at the bakery) proceed to visit Katerina Kittycat and her mother, Henrietta, to tell them about the special visitor coming. Katerina then comments, "A special meow meow visitor?" and in this way introduces readers to her signature verbal tic of inserting "meow meow" into the middle of phrases. Katerina suggests maybe the visitor is "supermommy," and she and Daniel imagine themselves as flying, caped superheroes on the following page.

Finally, nearly all the children and most of the other characters we've met gather at the Clock Factory at the center of town. King Friday announces that the visitor has arrived. The book reads, "Suddenly Daniel smiled. 'I see who the special visitor is' Daniel said with a cheer. He ran to greet the special visitor. Daniel wanted to be the first one to say hello. Who is the special visitor?" On the final page of the book, Daniel is pictured in a close-up, with his arms open wide and ready for a hug. "The special visitor is . . . YOU! Welcome to the neighborhood, neighbor! I'm so glad you're here. Ugga mugga!" In this way, the book directly addresses the reader (or the child being read to), much in the way that Daniel will occasionally directly address viewers of the television program.

More important in this context, this final page seeks to incorporate or include readers within the fictional world that has just been outlined on the previous pages. The book invites entry into this world, encouraging readers to explore "the neighborhood" further, especially now that the book has made readers aware of all the important locations, characters, and typical dramatic or stylistic conventions of the program. But exploring this "neighborhood" further actually involves consuming new texts and products; it requires that people engage with Daniel Tiger not just in the book but also in the television program, the numerous toys for sale at Target and Walmart, the various educational and entertainment apps made for iPads and other media platforms, or even a *Daniel Tiger Live* theatrical stage production that tours across the United States. *Welcome to the Neighborhood!* could easily go by another, more truthful title—"Welcome to the Franchise!"—as the book invites readers into a fictional world *and* into an intertextual network of cultural commodities. As the book encourages readers to engage with the Daniel Tiger world more broadly, one could argue that it is a kind of educational tool, training children how to enter into *any* fictional story world and participate with it through commercial products as well as creative play and thought. Just as the book and the animated show take place in a self-enclosed, coherent story world, the book and related texts take up mental space in readers and viewers. *Welcome to the Neighborhood!* informs readers about the world of Daniel Tiger but further teaches young readers or listeners how to create mental, imaginative space for franchised story worlds more generally.

Clearly, not all viewers of *Daniel Tiger's Neighborhood* will have read the book. But just as clearly, the book situates itself as an "entryway paratext," to borrow a phrase from Jonathan Gray (23, 35). As such, it invites consumers into an intertextual, industrial chain of products and solicits consumers to engage with these other texts and products. In ideal terms, this is how all franchised texts and products ought to work. Every text within a franchise can serve as an entryway; *Welcome to the Neighborhood!* just does so openly. Any appearance of Batman will link to all the others, and the same is true for Barbie, James Bond, Katniss Everdeen, Elsa of Arendelle, or Darth Vader. Any one of the texts or products in which these characters appear could lead a consumer to another and another, and that is precisely the hope of the people and companies that exploit and reexploit these intellectual properties.

At the same time, the individual texts and products within any film or media franchise are *modular* to varying degrees, meaning that they can be viewed or consumed independently from the others. In this respect, franchise texts and products are cogs and wheels within a larger franchise engine but still work all on their own. One need not have watched *CSI: Miami* (2002–2012) to watch and understand *CSI: NY* (2004–2013), for example, or to have watched the movie *Iron Man* (2008) to watch the television program *Marvel's Agents of S.H.I.E.L.D.* (2013–), even though these texts share the same story world. In other instances of this modular logic, a franchise may extend or continue while switching out different "cogs" or "wheels." Think, for instance, of the many different actors who have played James Bond or Batman. Or there is the case of the movie *XXX* (2002), in which Vin Diesel played the lead character, while the first sequel to the film (2005) featured actor Ice Cube playing a different character in the lead role, operating within the same fictional world as depicted in the earlier film. And while many children may gravitate toward backpacks and bandages that have pictures of Anna and Elsa because they have seen *Frozen* (2013), others may read books with these characters or dress up in costumes based on the movie without having seen it. Thus, although a franchise may entice consumers to explore additional texts and products and although a number of major franchises depict characters and narratives within a shared, internally logical and continuous story world, the individual instances of a franchise often stand far enough apart from the others that they can be consumed on their own. *Welcome to the Neighborhood!* is remarkable for working so blatantly to introduce *Daniel Tiger's Neighborhood* to readers, but the book is not *necessary* to engage with the Daniel Tiger franchise.

Having been introduced to Daniel Tiger and his friends with *Welcome to the Neighborhood!*, one might notice an interesting and commendable aspect of this story world and franchise. Namely, the characters living in *Daniel Tiger's Neighborhood* are somewhat diverse. Of course, a good number of the characters appear as cartoonish animals, allowing viewers to project onto them all sorts of social identities. But Miss Elaina lives in a multiracial family, for instance, as her father, Music Man Stan, is Black and her mother, Miss Elaine Fairchild, is white. Daniel's schoolteacher, Harriet, is also Black, and in one episode of the program, Daniel visits a female doctor who is South Asian. In addition to representing different races and ethnicities, *Daniel Tiger's Neighborhood* also depicts nonnormative family structures. Although there are no same-sex parents on the show, or LGBT-identified characters for that matter, Henrietta Pussycat appears to be raising

Katerina as a single mother, and O the Owl's guardian is his uncle.

Admittedly, it is a typical feature of many children's programs to feature nonwhite or otherwise socially diverse characters, such as in *Dora the Explorer* (2000–), *Doc McStuffins* (2012–), or *Sesame Street*. The diversity occurring in such programs extends in part from their cultural and educational ambitions. By the same token, however, we might also see the diversity appearing in *Daniel Tiger's Neighborhood* as yet another opening for multiple types of viewers or consumers to enter into these texts and products. The characters, relationships, and social situations that appear on this program provide multiple points of identification for a variety of viewers and consumers. To this extent, we might see the social diversity within the program aligning with the logic of extension and expansion occurring within the larger franchise.

We can see this dynamic playing out in a number of big, mainstream media franchises, and not only in kids programming. One of the most notable of these is the *Fast and Furious* franchise. The first of these films was released in 2001, and it tells the story of a white police officer, played by Paul Walker, going undercover within the underground car-racing scene in Los Angeles in order to infiltrate a gang that has been conducting high-speed robberies. The other main character, and foil to the undercover cop, is a street racer played by multiracial actor Vin Diesel. Additionally, Latina actress Michele Rodriguez plays the street racer's partner, and Rick Yune, who is of Korean descent, plays the main villain. Although it is a common trope within American action films to pair up "buddies" of different races, this first *Fast and Furious* film sets a precedent for multiracial, multiethnic ensemble casting that became one of the defining characteristics of the entire series. The second film, released in 2003, demonstrates the kind of modularity that is characteristic of many franchises, as it pairs Walker with African American actor Tyrese Gibson. The third film, taken on its own, is even more singular. Vin Diesel merely has a cameo at the end of the film, and Paul Walker does not appear at all. Instead, Lucas Black plays the protagonist in this multinational, multiracial ensemble piece; the movie takes place in Tokyo and features African American actor Bow Wow as well as a number of Japanese, Korean, Japanese American, and Korean American actors and actresses.

This series of films was firmly established as a globally popular franchise with the success of the fourth and fifth installments in 2009 and 2011, which featured the return of the original cast of Diesel, Walker, Rodriguez, and Jordana Brewster. By this time, however, Israeli actress Gal Godot and Black actor Dwayne Johnson had become recurring cast members, making Paul Walker merely one element in a multiracial, multiethnic, and multinational ensemble. In other words, these films did *not* present a situation in which there is a white "lead" and a nonwhite sidekick or buddy. Within the films themselves, as well, there is a discourse of inclusion and acceptance, which occurs as discussions about "family." Various characters regularly refer to their team of racers as constituting a family and claim that family is a virtue all its own and worth defending. Although there are real siblings within the team of heroes, most members are not blood related. As Vin Diesel's character states in *Furious 7* (2015), "I don't have friends, I have family." This discourse of "family" stands in as a way of claiming that racial, ethnic, and national differences do not hinder the creation of meaningful social bonds. The *Fast and Furious* films suggest, at the minimum, that social and cultural differences can be overcome or, to think of it less optimistically, conveniently overlooked.

Nevertheless, the *Fast and Furious* films exhibit an ideology of multiracial inclusion, with regard to their actual casting as well as within their narratives and dialogue. And global audiences demonstrate an acceptance of, or even an appetite for, action films with such representations, as these films have been immensely popular and financially successful in the United States and around the world. We might think, in fact, that part of these films' international appeal rests precisely on their approach toward social diversity. Mary Beltrán, for one, has asserted, "These cine-matic conventions clearly are in tune with contemporary sensibilities, as they characterize the now highly lucrative *Fast* franchise and a wide swath of films and television series in the past decade that have attempted to imitate its success" (95). Although Beltrán also acknowledges that there are limitations and contradictions within these films' racial and ethnic representational schemes (77), her point is well taken that these cultural texts resonate with our social and cultural world in such a way as to make them economically viable and even successful.

The *Paranormal Activity* series provides another case in which textual production is geared toward addressing different social identities. Yet, whereas the *Fast and Furious* films present diverse identities within each individual text, the case of *Paranormal Activity* displays a different strategy, in which textual production is oriented around one, specific ethnicity. The first in this series of "found footage" horror movies was released in 2007, after hav-ing played at the 2007 Screamfest Film Festival (Horn, "Biz"). Although the movie was made on a very small production budget, *Paranormal Activity* was extremely successful at the box office, earning nearly $200 million in theaters around the world ("Paranormal Activity"). This kind of low-budget success story followed in the wake of such similar horror films as *The Blair Witch Project*

(1999) and *Saw* (2004). Like those films, *Paranormal Activity* also kicked off a series of sequels and spin-offs that aimed to reexploit this now-established intellectual property. Indeed, the *Paranormal Activity* franchise presently consists of six films, helping to define the post-millennium horror-film genre alongside the *Insidious* and *Conjuring* franchises.

The first *Paranormal Activity* movie tells the story of a young couple who move into a large, suburban house in Southern California and quickly are beset by numerous spooky occurrences, such as objects moving on their own and lights turning on and off. The film depicts all this from video cameras that the man, Micah, sets up in the house. We discover that the woman, Katie, has been haunted by something her whole life, and this invisible demon attacks her with increasing ferocity as the film goes on. Eventually the movie ends with the demon possessing Katie and her murdering Micah. A closing text states that "Katie's whereabouts remain unknown," thus leaving the door open for her continued appearance in later films. And indeed, Katie appears in cameos in both *Paranormal Activity* 2 (2010) and 3 (2011), although these two movies tell alternative and "backstory" narratives. With *Paranormal Activity 4* (2012), we find that Katie has moved to Nevada, and she and the demon terrorize yet another, different family there.

In many respects, this series of films looks like any other successful horror-film series. Like Jason in the *Friday the 13th* movies, Michael Myers in the *Halloween* films, or Freddy Kruger in the *Nightmare on Elm Street* series, the character of Katie appears as *Paranormal Activity's* recurring antagonist. That is, although the series does provide an internally coherent, linked narrative world, the individual instances are only concretely linked by this one character and their shared *Paranormal Activity* title. I do not mean to suggest that *Paranormal Activity* is not really a franchise. Rather, I assert the opposite, that we might also see those other horror series in the context of media franchises. More significantly, film and media franchises are *generally* informed by the industrial and intertextual strategies occurring with low-budget horror films and other kinds of exploitation cinema. Although Derek Johnson is correct in seeing the beginnings of media franchises in retail and restaurant franchises, I claim that this is just *one* precursor to the current phenomenon.

For many years, horror and exploitation film producers consistently created sequel after sequel and remake after remake derived from the same idea or intellectual property. Doing so provided relative security within the volatile entertainment marketplace for the small-scale companies that produced such films. Just as important, the historically generally negative opinion regarding sequels and spin-offs can be linked to the abundance of low-budget sequels to horror films in particular (Jess-Cooke 53). To a significant degree, franchising merely entailed the rethinking of extremely similar business practices. The difference is twofold. First, as already detailed, franchises typically expand beyond one medium of representation and often into consumer merchandise as well. Second, and extending from the first, franchises typically create different versions of the same intellectual property in order to meet the desires of different consumer populations. In truth, franchises have gained a better (although still contentious) reputation in popular culture after this model of cultural production became the norm among the major Hollywood studios and after it informed an abundance of "mainstream" content, like kids media, blockbuster movies, and successful network programs.

One can see clearly the transition between these two models by looking briefly at *A Nightmare on Elm Street* (1984). The first film was an extremely bloody slasher film, and the success of this movie and its sequels prompted the copyright holder, New Line Cinema, to seek out different iterations of the Freddy Krueger character. By 1990, Freddy appeared on a syndicated television program (1988–1990) and a Nintendo video game. There were also Freddy Halloween costumes and a Freddy doll for kids, both of which were extremely popular (Ryan). Here, New Line Cinema altered and updated the kind of industrial intertextuality that would otherwise be typical of slasher films, with the production of sequels, to match the multimedia franchising logic that became so typical of big, mainstream media in the 1980s. Just as important, the franchising of Freddy Kruger in this fashion demonstrates how franchising logic often entails the creation of differ-ent texts and products specifically tailored to attract new or different consumer groups. In this particular instance, New Line aimed to make the Freddy Krueger character "child friendly" or at least acceptable as a toy. This seems quite ironic, considering that in the films' narratives Freddy is a child killer.

The *Paranormal Activity* franchise similarly expanded in such a way so as to engage a distinct audience group, although not in such a confused way as with *Nightmare on Elm Street*. A story in the *Los Angeles Times* spelled it out, stating, "Paramount Pictures' wildly successful horror movie franchise 'Paranormal Activity' gets a fourth super-natural spin this weekend, and if it follows the pattern of the earlier films, the box office will be bolstered by Latino moviegoers" (Horn, "In 'Paranormal'"). Consequently, as the article stated, "Just as Paramount starts bagging this weekend's windfall from 'Paranormal Activity 4,' the studio will begin production on a spinoff. . . . That film will be cast with Latino actors and aimed even more directly at that audience" (Horn, "In 'Paranormal' "). And, indeed, we get a glimpse of this franchise branching in a post-credits scene in *Paranormal Activity 4*. In it, we watch from the position of a handheld video camera as two men, who speak to each other in Spanish, enter a small shop on a busy street. Inside, we see shelves packed with an assortment of brightly colored goods, including an abundance of votive candles as well as a crucifix. A woman suddenly comes around the corner and states, "Esto es solo el comienzo" (this is only the beginning).

Thus, the fifth *Paranormal Activity* movie came out in 2014 under the title *Paranormal Activity: The Marked Ones* and featured a cast that was almost entirely Latino, and several passages in the film occur in untranslated Spanish. The film was set not in a large, new model, suburban home, as all the other films in the series had been, but instead took place in and around an apartment building in an urban neighborhood, thereby putting forth a certain understanding of where Latino people live. Although this film does feature narrative connections with the previous films, specifically by linking to the villainess Katie, it functions relatively independently, too. Audiences can explain some of what they see by linking this film's narrative to the previous films, but it is not necessary that they have seen those films. More directly, we can take the title of this film as an indication of its singularity; whereas all the other films simply differentiated themselves with a number (*Paranormal Activity 2, 3,* etc.), *The Marked Ones* suggests a deviation significant enough that it merits an entirely new designation. And film critics, in both positive and negative reviews, treated this movie as a variance. One critic called it "a parenthetical between 'Paranormal Activity 4' (2012) and the upcoming 'Paranormal Activity 5'" (Keough), and another stated that the film "feels like a fresh start," after having discussed the difference of this film's title in relation to the other films in the series (Olsen).

As an overtly modular entry into the *Paranormal Activity* franchise, *The Marked Ones* is notable for the self-conscious, deliberate way in which it attempts to engage Latino audiences. Although the film was less successful than previous entries into the series were, it is difficult to say whether this was a result of its demographic strategy or simply because audiences of all types were less interested in the film's premise or the larger franchise. (Notably, the film that followed this one in the series, *Paranormal Activity: The Ghost Dimension* [2015], was even less successful.) More important, *The Marked Ones* demonstrates how the drive toward expansion within franchise logic led to the production of a movie oriented toward a specific social identity. Whereas something like the *Fast and Furious* films represent diverse ensembles *within* each film, we can see the *Paranormal Activity* franchise as constituting a somewhat diverse ensemble through the collection of films as a whole. As an example, then, *Paranormal Activity* in general and *The Marked Ones* in particular show how the segments or modules within a franchise can seek to address or align with the different segments within our culture.

At this point, in fact, there are numerous film and media franchises that appear aimed at distinct audiences, without necessarily looking to expand by directly appealing to other groups of consumers. After the novel *Sex and the City* was published in 1997, for example, it was adapted into a highly successful television series on HBO (1998–2004). This series focused on the lives of four women in New York and was especially popular with female viewers. The success of the series led to the production of two movies, *Sex and the City* (2008) and *Sex and the City 2* (2010), as well as another book, *The Carrie Diaries*, which was published in 2010 and served as a "prequel" to the previous texts and which was subsequently adapted into yet another television series that aired on the CW network (2013–2014). Although *The Carrie Diaries* sought to engage younger consumers by featuring an adolescent version of the series' protagonist, all of the *Sex and the City* texts were explicitly aimed at female audiences.

Analogously, producer, director, and actor Tyler Perry has made a remarkable number of successful plays, films, and television programs featuring Black performers and aimed at African American audiences. Many of Perry's texts are comedies and feature the character Madea, such as the movies *Diary of a Mad Black Woman* (2005) and *A Madea Christmas* (2013). Although some people have criticized Perry's works and their representations of African Americans, his plays, television programs, and movies have consistently been popular with Black audiences (and others) and very economically successful, making him a prominent figure in American media. Thus, in cases like *Sex and the City* and the works of Tyler Perry, we see that certain media franchises engage with the issue of social diversity by appealing to specific identity groups and less with others. Franchises like these may not expand through creating new products for different populations but nevertheless work to address the social diversity that characterizes the larger arena of popular media culture.

Before we get too satisfied with the ways in which some media franchises intersect with our diverse culture, however, we need to remember several factors that complicate or even undermine this situation. First, we should understand that although a film, television program, or other media text might represent a diverse cast of characters, in many cases such texts do not engage in any meaningful way with the ways in which social identities are constructed and experienced. In fact, rather than contending with gender, race, ethnicity, or sexuality in a concrete or thoughtful way, many popular media texts situate characters within narratives and situations where issues of social difference can be overlooked due to the internal logic of the story world, such as with many fantasy and science-fiction films. Further, we know that simply because a media text features performers with different skin tones or accents, it does not mean that this representation is not demeaning or patronizing. As Kristen Warner has written regarding race and ethnicity in particular, "the idea of contemporary ethnic representation in media today seems only to concern quantity and not necessarily quality" (6). Indeed, we might see many examples in which a media text or product aims at a social identity group and does so in an ignorant fashion.

Second, it is important to note that media products can be watched and enjoyed by all manner of people, no matter what kinds of performers and characters appear in these texts. Many white girls adore *Doc McStuffins*, many men enjoy the witty dialogue of *The Gilmore Girls* (2000–2007), and as the example of *Paranormal Activity* made clear, many Latino viewers enjoyed watching white people get terrorized by demons before Paramount made *The Marked Ones*. Just because a franchise or text *appears* to aim for a specific audience or consumer group, it does not mean that it is limited to being consumed or enjoyed by that group.

This point raises the third factor that complicates franchise "enfranchisement," namely, that it remains the case that some of the biggest, most prominent, most popular media franchises are overwhelmingly white centered and male driven. We see this most recently in such franchise movies as *Batman v. Superman: Dawn of Justice* (2016), *Jurassic World* (2015), *The Hobbit: The Battle of the Five Armies* (2014), and *Transformers: Age of Extinction* (2014); the list goes on. Of course, not all viewers of these films, or consumers of the products based on these movies, were white or male. Yet the texts themselves compelled all sorts of viewers, from all over the world, to engage with the drama of white, male protagonists or character ensembles. Examples like these make it clear that, although some franchises are sensitive or commercially savvy enough to engage with social diversity, much of mainstream popular media persists in upholding white and masculine perspectives and points of identification.

At the same time that it appears that audiences around the world can and do respond positively to franchises that appeal to social diversity, there are people and groups in the world that resist and push back against the franchises that do not. As a writer for the *Christian Science Monitor* observed, for instance, "The seeming reluctance to invest in female-led superhero films has angered many fans," and she also noted, "Scarlett Johansson has portrayed superhero Black Widow four times . . . and fans have been calling for her to have her own movie for some time now" (Lindsay). One can also look to the website The Hawkeye Initiative to see fans resisting the misogyny that endures in comic books and superhero movies. Here, fans take comic book covers and artwork that features a supposedly "strong" female character and replace this figure with the superhero Hawkeye. In doing so, these fan artworks make clear the sexism that informs the drawing of female characters, as Hawkeye now appears bizarre as he arches his back to thrust out his chest, curves his hips and buttocks, or otherwise takes up limp, flailing, or supple poses.

As a final example, we can look to the widespread responses to the release of a *Star Wars*–themed version of the Monopoly board game. Although players could use a variety of *Star Wars* characters as pieces within the game, including Darth Vader and Luke Skywalker, the protagonist from *The Force Awakens*, Rey, was not included as an option (Leane). Fans were so upset about Rey's absence from this game, as well as from other *Force Awakens* toys and games, that they started an internet campaign called

"Where's Rey?" asking for Disney and toy company Hasbro to release more Rey products (Cunha). This action seems to have had some effect, as it prompted Hasbro to release a response, which stated, "Fans will see more Rey product hitting store shelves. . . . We are thrilled with the popularity of this compelling character and will continue to look for ways to showcase Rey across all of our product lines" (Leane).

Incidents and responses like these demonstrate how social diversity within popular, commercial media remains a highly contested and contentious issue. It certainly appears that a remarkable number of media franchises are contending with social difference, in a variety of ways and to varying degrees of success. In some cases, this practice simply seeks to draw different consumer groups toward the same core intellectual property. Teens and adults may watch *Batman v. Superman*, while kids may watch *Justice League Action* (2016–), and little girls may play with "DC Superhero Girls" action figures; all of these texts and products derive from Warner Bros.' hold on the intellectual property for all of the related DC comic book characters. In other ways, though, we see that the drive to represent a variety of different kinds of people can lead to new and potentially empowering forms of creativity within a franchise. Think of *The Force Awakens* or the *Fast and Furious* movies or even something like *Mad*

Max: Fury Road (2015), in which the ostensible protagonist, Max, appears to be almost a secondary character to the powerful, decision-making protagonist, Furiosa, played by Charlize Theron, and her band of female slaves-turned-warriors. It is true that film and media franchises saturate popular culture with repetitious appearances of characters, story worlds, and even ideas and ideologies. But in this process, there are glimmers of hope that the *variations* within these franchises can offer some new, more inclusive representations of the great diversity that defines our contemporary social world.

CONCLUSION
The Importance of Film Remakes and Franchises

What makes film remakes and media franchises so important? Is it because they appear to dominate contemporary media culture? Is it because the Hollywood studios and other major media companies rely on recycling old texts and existing intellectual properties in order to reduce the economic "risks" of cultural production? Is it because audiences respond so strongly to remakes and franchises, returning to watch and rewatch familiar stories, with established characters, in recognizable story worlds?

Remakes and franchises are not important simply because they are so prevalent, as there is nothing at all new about the recycling of existing texts, characters, or story worlds. But all of the factors just listed do contribute to the cultural significance of film remakes and franchises. Media producers and distributors *do* rely on their ownership, exploitation, and reexploitation of select intellectual properties; creatively using and producing works based on intellectual property constitutes their core business, in fact. By drawing from the same pool of ideas, characters, and stories, media companies are able to orient their production activities and regulate the commercial market for entertainment products. To a considerable extent, film and media producers actively define what they do by deliberately endeavoring to make remakes and franchises. And on the flip side, film critics, media audiences, and cultural consumers orient their own thoughts about, responses to, and discussions of popular media in relation to remakes and franchises. Indeed, critics and audiences have defined the very idea of remakes to a significant degree. As cultural categories, "remakes" and "franchises" help us sort through, understand, appreciate, and critique a significant amount of the media we encounter every day.

That is, film remakes and franchises are important because they shape and orient how so much contemporary media is produced and consumed. As products of industrial intertextuality, remakes and franchises do not simply create connections among different films, television programs, video games, and countless other cultural texts and consumer goods. They link media producers and consumers to one another in the great, interwoven network of texts and discourses we call "culture," with all of these groups straining to mark their own significance through the relationships they forge with each other through these texts. Yes, film remakes and franchises currently appear to dominate popular culture. Yes, the abundance of remakes and franchises can make media culture appear highly derivative and repetitious. And yes, all of these texts represent the work of a limited number of companies, which profit from their exclusive ownership over so many characters and stories that we all (somewhat mistakenly) think of as "ours." Yet, at the same time, remakes and franchises represent the creative, cultural forms that so many people seek out, enjoy, consider, respond to, and integrate within their daily lives and even their imaginations. Within this historical moment, remakes and franchises represent something like an agreement between media producers and consumers about how cultural products should appear and circulate. And although the terms of this agreement are not evenly balanced or fair, we have seen that critics, audiences, and consumers are not powerless in shaping their responses to, or even their definitions of, these forms of industrial intertextuality. Remakes and franchise texts are commercial entertainment products, to be sure, but they have significance only because audiences remain committed to consuming and responding creatively to them.

If this characterization of the role that film remakes and franchises play in popular culture seems optimistic or celebratory, make no mistake—I think we all need to be highly critical of the ways in which our "popular" culture is shaped by commercial interests. Like many people, I sometimes roll my eyes when I hear that, say, another *Spiderman* movie is in the works or shake my head when I see an entire aisle at Target devoted to *Finding Dory* (2016) toys. Hopefully, though, this book has provided some tools that might be used by readers to formulate their own critical thoughts and responses to remakes and franchises. Simply sorting through, defining, and providing examples of some of the most common and noteworthy forms of intertextuality that we encounter in popular culture can help us begin to understand how complex all of these cultural forms actually are. By providing a basic vocabulary of the many forms of industrial intertextuality, we can begin to assess what these forms mean to us and to the larger world in which we live and participate as citizens.

Similarly, by looking closely at and analyzing film remakes, we can gain a better appreciation for these films, if only because we can then refute a few of the common misconceptions about them. Film remakes are not a new phenomenon, as they began occurring at nearly the same moment that cinema was invented. Film remakes are not more abundant now than they were in the past, as we saw that filmmakers engaged in a deluge of copying in the early part of the twentieth century. And film remakes are not necessarily "worse" than the films on which they are based, as some cases prove that filmmakers can innovate film form and storytelling technique at the same time that they borrow from the plot of an earlier film. More important, though, we have to wonder *how* and *by whom* a remake's quality gets assessed and what the motivations and consequences are for the critics and audiences who make such judgments. But how are we to evaluate a film remake's qualities and significance while still setting aside judgments of "good," "bad," "better," or "worse"? By looking "back" and "across," we can all better understand why any particular remake looks the way it does and evaluate how it "fits" (or does not fit) within its particular cultural context.

The present cultural context seems especially defined by the presences of media franchises and the industrial process of media franchising. Although we do still encounter the occasional "traditional" remake, with something like *True Grit* (2010), which aims to retell the story from an earlier film (1969) but which does not aim for additional narrative extensions, it seems more and more remakes are actually reboots that strive to kick off a chain of related texts and products. We see this with the new *Power Rangers* (2017) and *Tomb Raider* (2018) movies, among others. Given the way that franchises aim to spread across texts, media platforms, and consumer products, they can feel ubiquitous and even overwhelming, making it difficult to assess what they mean or what makes them important. But we can remember several aspects of media franchises that, at minimum, suggest their complexity and allure. First, franchises require a lot of work, and the process of franchising a single intellectual property across texts and products often entails the coordination of multiple cultural producers, including film companies, television distributors, game and toy manufacturers, and retailers, to name a few. As a system that entails both an industrial *and* an intertextual network, the complexity of media franchises actually makes them quite delicate, requiring consistent labor on the part of media companies to maintain their relationships with one another and sustain the interest of fans. Likewise, franchises require the work of so many consumers, to forge the links among these texts and products in their minds and, in practice, with their consumption habits.

Second, film and media franchises can offer opportunities for representations of and engagements with the social and cultural diversity that characterizes the world in which we live. We can, and probably should, lament the fact that franchises are driven by the desire of various companies and corporations to capitalize on their strict holds on certain intellectual properties. But in their very pursuit to extend themselves and attract new consumers, a remarkable number of franchises incorporate characters from a variety of racial, ethnic, gendered, and generational affiliations, offering portraits of social diversity at the same time that they provide multiple or diverse points of identification. The enfranchisement offered by media franchises to different social groups may seem like a debased form of participation in society; consumption is no replacement for citizenship. But given that so much of popular culture occurs as commercial entertainment, it seems limited and even wrongheaded not to acknowledge and perhaps appreciate these efforts to make media texts and consumer products that are responsive to a diverse variety of people and social groups.

As a final note, I should say something about creativity and fun. The repetitive and derivative nature of remakes and franchise texts might signal a lack of original thought or artistic innovation. But it remains the case that all of art and culture is repetitive and derivative of the art and culture that came before. Remakes and franchise texts just carry the burden of their overt, often announced connection to other texts, and to this extent, they invite comparative assessments. And works like these do allow for forms of innovation and creativity, within the bounds of intellectual property law, of course, and we see these works make novel variations and adjustments on characters, character types, stories, and story worlds. The repetition *and variation* within media texts appear to be what lures and excites audiences time and time again. So while I may roll my eyes or shake my head at commercial media on occasion, I continue to be intrigued, thrilled, saddened, charmed, and generally *moved* by a great number of movies, television programs, and other media texts and products—including many film remakes and franchises. Remakes and franchise texts can be a lot of fun. My hope here has been to show that it can also be fun to analyze them, to better understand how they work, and to appreciate what makes them significant within our culture.

ACKNOWLEDGMENTS

I have been thinking about remakes, adaptations, and other forms of cinematic intertextuality since 2002. It is therefore impossible to thank all of the friends and colleagues who have shaped and supported my work on this topic in the short space provided here. Instead, I will simply mention a few of the significant influences on this book. Bill Whittington had me as a teaching assistant in his "Adaptations" class at USC and generously provided me the space to develop my own ideas on this subject; much of that early thinking has morphed into the present work. Marsha Kinder oversaw my dissertation on the subject of transnational film remakes and was supremely helpful regarding my thinking about intertextuality. Just one amazing conversation with Anne Friedberg still guides my thoughts about remakes.

I am grateful also to Constantine Verevis, for writing such inspiring works about film remakes and also, more crucially, for his early and continuing support of my scholarship. Similarly, I have admired the work of Derek Johnson and Jonathan Gray for some time, and I am glad to count them as friends. Various conversations with Derek and Jonathan helped me sort through my own thoughts about franchises and paratexts. Erin Hanna deserves special thanks for reading and providing commentary on this entire manuscript. I deeply appreciate the time and careful thought she devoted to my work; there are few people whose expertise I trust more on this topic. Chuck Tryon provided peerless peer-review commentary on this book for the press, and his suggestions were characteristically thoughtful and productive; I admire Chuck a lot, and I was fortunate to have him as my reader. As always, I am indebted to Dana Polan for his intellectual guidance and professional mentorship; the creativity and range of his critical thinking provides a model I hope to emulate.

At the University of Michigan, Phil Hallman has been as great a friend as he has been a librarian. I am also thankful for all the encouragement I have gotten from my colleagues, including Richard Abel, Megan Ankerson, Giorgio Bertellini, Jim Burnstein, Hugh Cohen, Victor Fanucchi, Caryl Flinn, Colin Gunckel, Dawn Hollison, Mark Kligerman, Amanda Lotz, David Marek, Chris McNamara, Sheila Murphy, Sarah Murray, Lisa Nakamura, Markus Nornes, Aswin Punathambekar, Yeidy Rivero, Terri Sarris, Katherine Sender, Matthew Solomon, and Johannes von Moltke. Nothing in my professional life would happen without the kind help from the staff in the Department of Screen Arts & Cultures, and I am extremely thankful for all the assistance provided by Mary Lou Chlipala, Carrie Moore, Lisa Rohde, and Marga Schuhwerk-Hampel.

I also wish to thank Wheeler Winston Dixon for bringing up the possibility of writing this book, and he and Gwendolyn Audrey Foster have been wonderfully supportive and insightful in helping me bring it to completion. Likewise, Leslie Mitchner has been a truly fantastic editor, and I am thrilled that I was able to work with her. I am grateful for her sharp and critical eye as well as her profound understanding of the writing process and the publishing landscape. Many thanks also to Andrew Katz for his excellent copyediting work and to Victoria Baker, indexer extraordinaire.

Many friends and family members were supportive and helpful in all sorts of ways as I have bounced around ideas about remakes over the years. My late father, Patrick Daniel Herbert, would have loved the intellectual puzzle presented by remakes and franchises, and I am thankful for his guidance and the continuing support of my stepmother, Liz Buckner. My mother, Susan Cogar, is perpetually helpful, as is my stepfather, Ron Cogar. I am grateful to my brothers, Charles and Noel, for all the fun and conversations, and to Charles's wife, Larissa, as well. My in-laws, Gary and Karla Sampson, have been exceptionally encouraging and supportive, and John Sampson and Carmelita Parraz have been wonderful. A special thanks to Cass and Deanna Cook, who let me use their amazing cabin where I wrote the introduction and chapter 1 of this book. My unending gratitude and love goes to Anna Sampson, who has been so generous and loving through everything. And finally, thanks to Clara Tarryall Herbert for introducing me to Daniel Tiger and for reintroducing me to everything else that is wonderful in life.

FURTHER READING

Altman, Rick. *Film/Genre*. London: BFI, 1999.

Barthes, Roland. *Image-Music-Text*. Trans. Stephen Heath. New York: Hill and Wang, 1977.

Bennett, Tony, and Jane Woollacott. *Bond and Beyond: The Political Career of a Popular Hero*. London: Macmillan Education, 1987.

Corrigan, Timothy. *Film and Literature: An Introduction and Reader*. 2nd ed. New York: Routledge, 2011.

Decherney, Peter. *Hollywood's Copyright Wars: From Edison to the Internet*. New York: Columbia University Press, 2012.

Druxman, Michael. *Make It Again, Sam: A Survey of Movie Remakes*. South Brunswick, NJ: A. S. Barnes, 1975.

Durham, Carolyn. *Double Takes: Culture and Gender in French Films and Their American Remakes*. Hanover, NH: University Press of New England, 1998.

Eco, Umberto. *The Limits of Interpretation*. Bloomington: Indiana University Press, 1990.

Elsaesser, Thomas. "The Blockbuster: Everything Connects, but Not Everything Goes." *The End of Cinema as We Know It*. Ed. Jon Lewis. New York: NYU Press, 2001. 11–22.

Forrest, Jennifer, ed. *The Legend Returns and Dies Harder Another Day: Essays on Film Series*. Jefferson, NC: McFarland, 2008.

Forrest, Jennifer, and Leonard R. Koos, eds. *Dead Ringers: The Remake in Theory and Practice*. Albany: State University of New York Press, 2002.

Genette, Gérard. *Palimpsests: Literature in the Second Degree.* Trans. Channa Newman and Claude Dubinsky. Lincoln: University of Nebraska Press, 1997.

Gray, Jonathan. *Show Sold Separately: Promos, Spoilers, and Other Media Paratexts*. New York: NYU Press, 2010.

———. *Watching "The Simpsons": Television, Parody, and Intertextuality*. New York: Routledge, 2006.

Harries, Dan. *Film Parody*. London: BFI, 2000.

Heinze, Rüdiger, and Lucia Krämer, eds. *Remakes and Remaking: Concepts—Media—Practices*. Bielefeld, Germany: Transcript Verlag, 2015.

Herbert, Daniel. "*Sky*'s the Limit: Transnationality and Identity in *Abre los Ojos* and *Vanilla Sky*." *Film Quarterly* 60.1 (2006): 28–38.

———. "Transnational Film Remakes: Time, Space, Identity." PhD diss., University of Southern California, 2008.

Horton, Andrew, and Stuart Y. McDougal, eds. *Play It Again, Sam: Retakes on Remakes*. Berkeley: University of California Press, 1998.

Hutcheon, Linda. *A Theory of Adaptation*. New York: Routledge, 2006.

Iampolski, Mikhail. *The Memory of Tiresias: Intertextuality and Film*. Trans. Harsha Ram. Berkeley: University of California Press, 1998.

Jenkins, Henry. *Convergence Culture: Where Old and New Media Collide*. Cambridge, MA: MIT Press, 2006.

———. *Textual Poachers: Television Fans and Participatory Culture.* New York: Routledge, 1992.

Jess-Cooke, Carolyn. *Film Sequels.* Edinburgh: Edinburgh University Press, 2009.

Jess-Cooke, Carolyn, and Constantine Verevis, eds. *Second Takes: Critical Approaches to the Film Sequel.* Albany: State University of New York Press, 2010.

Johnson, Derek. *Media Franchising: Creative License and Collaboration in the Cultural Industries.* New York: NYU Press, 2013.

Kinder, Marsha. *Playing with Power in Movies, Television, and Video Games: From Muppet Babies to Teenage Mutant Ninja Turtles.* Berkeley: University of California Press, 1991.

Klein, Amanda Ann, and R. Barton Palmer, eds. *Cycles, Sequels, Spin-offs, Remakes, and Reboots: Multiplicities in Film and Television.* Austin: University of Texas Press, 2016.

Kristeva, Julia. *Desire in Language: A Semiotic Approach to Literature and Art.* New York: Columbia University Press, 1980.

Lavigne, Carlen, ed. *Remake Television: Reboot, Re-use, Recycle.* Lanham, MA: Lexington Books, 2014.

Leitch, Thomas. *Film Adaptation and Its Discontents: From "Gone with the Wind" to "The Passion of the Christ."* Baltimore: Johns Hopkins University Press, 2007.

Limbacher, James L. *Haven't I Seen You Somewhere Before? Remakes, Sequels, and Series in Motion Pictures and Television, 1896–1978.* New York: Pierian, 1991.

Loock, Kathleen, and Constantine Verevis, eds. *Film Remakes, Adaptations, and Fan Productions: Remake/Remodel*. New York: Palgrave Macmillan, 2012.

Lukas, Scott A., and John Marmysz, eds. *Fear, Cultural Anxiety, and Transformation: Horror, Science Fiction, and Fantasy Films Remade*. Lanham, MD: Lexington Books, 2009.

Marshall, P. David. "The New Intertextual Commodity." *The New Media Book*. Ed. Dan Harries. London: BFI, 2002. 69–81.

Mazdon, Lucy. *Encore Hollywood: Remaking French Cinema*. London: BFI, 2000.

Mittell, Jason. *Genre and Television: From Cop Shows to Cartoons in American Culture*. New York: Routledge, 2004.

Naremore, James, ed. *Film Adaptations*. New Brunswick, NJ: Rutgers University Press, 2000.

Nowlan, Robert, and Gwendolyn Wright Nowlan. *Cinema Sequels and Remakes, 1903–1987*. Jefferson, NC: McFarland, 1989.

Perkins, Claire, and Constantine Verevis, eds. *Film Trilogies: New Critical Approaches*. New York: Palgrave Macmillan, 2012.

———, eds. *Transnational Television Remakes*. London: Routledge, 2016.

Proctor, William. "Regeneration & Rebirth: An Anatomy of the Franchise Reboot." *Scope: An Online Journal of Film and Television Studies*, no. 22 (February 2012): 1–19. www.nottingham.ac.uk/scope/documents/2012/february-2012/proctor.pdf.

Santo, Avi. *Selling the Silver Bullet: The Lone Ranger and Transmedia Brand Licensing*. Austin: University of Texas Press. 2015.

Smith, Iain Robert, and Constantine Verevis, eds. *Transnational Film Remakes*. Edinburgh: Edinburgh University Press, 2017.

Stam, Robert. *Literature through Film: Realism, Magic, and the Art of Adaptation*. Malden, MA: Blackwell, 2004.

Stam, Robert, and Alessandra Raengo, eds. *Literature and Film: A Guide to the Theory and Practice of Film Adaptation*. Malden, MA: Blackwell, 2005.

Thompson, Kristin. *The Frodo Franchise: "The Lord of the Rings" and Modern Hollywood*. Berkeley: University of California Press, 2007.

Tryon, Chuck. "Reboot Cinema." *Convergence: The International Journal of Research into New Media Technologies* 19.4 (2013): 423–437.

Varndell, Daniel. *Hollywood Remakes, Deleuze, and the Grandfather Paradox*. New York: Palgrave Macmillan, 2014.

Verevis, Constantine. *Film Remakes*. Edinburgh: Edinburgh University Press, 2006.

Wang, Yiman. *Remaking Chinese Cinema: Through the Prism of Shanghai, Hong Kong, and Hollywood*. Honolulu: University of Hawai'i Press, 2013.

Warner, Kristen J. *The Cultural Politics of Colorblind TV Casting*. New York: Routledge, 2015.

Wee, Valerie. *Japanese Horror Films and Their American Remakes: Translating Fear, Adapting Culture*. New York: Routledge, 2014.

Wees, William. *Recycled Images: The Art and Politics of Found Footage Films.* New York: Anthology Film Archives, 1993.

Zanger, Anat. *Film Remakes as Ritual and Disguise.* Amsterdam: Amsterdam University Press, 2006.

WORKS CITED

Abel, Richard. *The Ciné Goes to Town: French Cinema, 1896–1914*. Updated and expanded ed. Berkeley: University of California Press, 1994.

Andrew, Dudley. "Adaptation." *Film Adaptations*. Ed. James Naremore. New Brunswick, NJ: Rutgers University Press. 28–37.

Barthes, Roland. "From Work to Text." *Image-Music-Text*. Trans. Stephen Heath. New York: Hill and Wang, 1977. 155–164.

Beltrán, Mary. "Fast and Bilingual: *Fast & Furious* and the Latinization of Racelessness." *Cinema Journal* 53.1 (2013): 75–96.

Brew, Simon. "RoboCop Reboot: Sequel Plans Not Dead." Den of Geek 11 Sept. 2015. www.denofgeek.com/movies/robocop/36897/robocop-reboot-sequel-plans-not-dead.

Buchanan, Judith. *Shakespeare on Silent Film: An Excellent Dumb Discourse*. Cambridge: Cambridge University Press, 2009.

Burr, Ty. "'Carrie' Is a Dispiriting Remake of Horror Classic." *Boston Globe* 18 Oct. 2013.

Carr, Jay. "Caruso Sears in Savage, Savvy 'Kiss.'" *Boston Globe* 21 Apr. 1995.

Chapman, Seymour. "What Novels Can Do That Films Can't (and Vice Versa)." *Critical Inquiry* 7.1 (1980): 121–140.

Cieply, Michael. "Disney Is Buying Lucasfilm for $4 Billion." *New York Times* 31 Oct. 2012.

Cole, Bruce. *The Renaissance Artist at Work: From Pisano to Titian*. New York: Harper and Row, 1983.

Copernicus. "Copernicus Saw THE MARTIAN at TIFF, and Has Round 2 of SCIENCE VS. CINEMA." Ain't It Cool News 14 Sept. 2015. www.aintitcool.com/node/73045.

Cunha, Darlena. "'Where's Rey' Proves Kids Are Light Years Ahead of Toy Companies." *Time* 7 Jan. 2016. http://time.com/4170424/star-wars-wheres-rey.

Dargis, Manohla, and A. O. Scott. "The Year the Studios Got It Right." *New York Times* 1 Jan. 2016. www.nytimes .com/2016/01/03/movies/the-year-the-studios-get-it -right.html?_r=0.

Deadline Team, The. "Comic-Con: Legendary Unveils Glimpse of New King Kong Pic 'Skull Island.'" *Deadline Hollywood* 26 July 2014. http://deadline.com/2014/07/ king-kong-skull-island-movie-legendary-810372.

Decherney, Peter. *Hollywood's Copyright Wars: From Edison to the Internet*. New York: Columbia University Press, 2012.

"Feel-Good Flick, A." *Grand Rapids Press* 1 Oct. 1999.

Fleming, Mike, Jr. "Warner Bros Sets King Kong vs Godzilla, as Deadline Told You Last Month." *Deadline Hollywood* 14 Oct. 2015. http://deadline.com/2015/10/king-kong -godzilla-warner-bros-legendary-pictures-1201582155.

Forrest, Jennifer. Introduction. *The Legend Returns and Dies Harder Another Day: Essays on Film Series*. Ed. Jennifer Forrest. Jefferson, NC: McFarland, 2008. 1–19.

——. "The 'Personal' Touch: The Original, the Remake, and the Dupe in Early Cinema." *Dead Ringers: The Remake in Theory and Practice*. Ed. Jennifer Forrest and Leonard R. Koos. Albany: State University of New York Press, 2002. 89–126.

Friedman, Becky. *Welcome to the Neighborhood!* New York: Simon Spotlight / Simon and Schuster, 2014.

Fritz, Ben. "Souping Up a Film Franchise." *Los Angeles Times* 26 Apr. 2011.

Goodman, Nelson. *Languages of Art: An Approach to a Theory of Symbols*. Indianapolis: Bobbs-Merrill, 1968.

Gray, Jonathan. *Show Sold Separately: Promos, Spoilers, and Other Media Paratexts*. New York: NYU Press, 2010.

Gunning, Tom. "The Cinema of Attraction: Early Film, Its Spectator and the Avant-Garde." *Wide Angle* 8.3 (1986): 63–70.

——. *D. W. Griffith and the Origins of American Narrative Film: The Early Years at Biograph*. Urbana: University of Illinois Press, 1991.

——. "The Intertextuality of Early Cinema: A Prologue to *Fantômas*, Film and Novel." *The Legend Returns and Dies Harder Another Day: Essays on Film Series*. Ed. Jennifer Forrest. Jefferson, NC: McFarland, 2008. 39–56.

Harries, Dan. *Film Parody*. London: BFI, 2000.

Herbert, Daniel. "*Sky*'s the Limit: Transnationality and Identity in *Abre los Ojos* and *Vanilla Sky*." *Film Quarterly* 60.1 (2006): 28–38.

——. "Transnational Film Remakes: Time, Space, Identity." PhD diss., University of Southern California, 2008.

Horn, John. "The Biz: The Film That Jolted Spielberg into 'Yes.'" *Los Angeles Times* 20 Sept. 2009.

———. "In 'Paranormal,' Thrills Translate: Latinos Have Been Big Fans of the Horror Franchise. Paramount Is Counting on It." *Los Angeles Times* 18 Oct. 2012.

Horrorella. "Horrorella Takes One for the Team and Reviews the *Cabin Fever* Remake!" Ain't It Cool News 13 Feb. 2016. www.aintitcool.com/node/74447.

Hustad, Karis. "RoboCop Gets a 2014 Reboot: Will It Work?" *Christian Science Monitor* 9 Sept. 2013. www.csmonitor.com/Technology/2013/0909/RoboCop-gets-a-2014-reboot-Will-it-work.

Hutcheon, Linda. *A Theory of Adaptation*. New York: Routledge, 2006.

Jameson, Fredric. *Postmodernism, or, The Cultural Logic of Late Capitalism*. Durham, NC: Duke University Press, 1991.

Jenkins, Henry. *Convergence Culture: Where Old and New Media Collide*. Cambridge, MA: MIT Press, 2006.

———. *Textual Poachers: Television Fans and Participatory Culture*. New York: Routledge, 1992.

Jess-Cooke, Carolyn. *Film Sequels*. Edinburgh: Edinburgh University Press, 2009.

Johnson, Derek. *Media Franchising: Creative License and Collaboration in the Cultural Industries*. New York: NYU Press, 2013.

Keegan, Rebecca. "'Star Wars: The Force Awakens' Reflects Our Diverse, Modern World." *Los Angeles Times* 21 Dec. 2015.

Keough, Peter. "Very Little Is New in Latest 'Paranormal Activity.'" *Boston Globe* 6 Jan. 2014.

Kinder, Marsha. *Playing with Power in Movies, Television, and Video Games: From Muppet Babies to Teenage Mutant Ninja Turtles*. Berkeley: University of California Press, 1991.

Kingsley, Grace. "Film Remakes Found Unwise." *Los Angeles Times* 10 Apr. 1931.

Kirst, Seamus. "With Diverse Characters, 'The Force Awakens' Has Great Success While Practicing Inclusive Casting." *Forbes* 21 Dec. 2015.

Leane, Rob. "Star Wars: Hasbro Promises More Rey in Future Products." Den of Geek! 6 Jan. 2016. www.denof geek.com/movies/star-wars/38418/star-wars-hasbro -promises-more-rey-in-future-products.

Leitch, Thomas. "Twice Told Tales: Disavowal and the Rhetoric of the Remake." *Dead Ringers: The Remake in Theory and Practice*. Ed. Jennifer Forrest and Leonard R. Koos. Albany: State University of New York Press, 2002. 37–62.

Lieberman, David. "Hollywood Retreads Have 'Played Out,' Endangering Profits: Analyst." Deadline Hollywood 24 Sept. 2015. http://deadline.com/2015/09/studio-use -sequels-retreads-played-out-box-office-1201548117.

Lindsay, Rowena. "Is It Time for a Female-Led Superhero Film?" *Christian Science Monitor* 5 May 2015.

Loiperdinger, Martin, and Bernd Elzer. "Lumière's *Arrival of the Train*: Cinema's Founding Myth." *Moving Image* 4.1 (2004): 89–118.

Loock, Kathleen. "Retro-Remaking: The 1980s Film Cycle in Contemporary Hollywood Cinema." *Cycles, Sequels, Spin-offs, Remakes, and Reboots: Multiplicities in Film and Television*. Ed. Amanda Ann Klein and R. Barton Palmer. Austin: University of Texas Press, 2016. 277–298.

Maslin, Janet. "Styron's 'Sophie's Choice.'" *New York Times* 10 Dec. 1982.

McIntyre, Gina. "A Rad Pitch to Reboot a Classic." *Los Angeles Times* 2 Feb. 2014.

Means, Sean P. "Curtis, Lohan Bring the Magic to a Warm Remake of 'Freaky Friday.'" *Salt Lake Tribune* 6 Aug. 2003.

Meehan, Eileen. "'Holy Commodity Fetish, Batman!': The Political Economy of a Commercial Intertext." *The Many Lives of the Batman: Critical Approaches to a Superhero and His Media*. Ed. Roberto Pearson and William Uricchio. New York: Routledge, 2004. 47–65.

Miller, Barbara. "New Editions of Old Films Stir Debate." *Los Angeles Times* 4 Apr. 1937.

Mittell, Jason. *Genre and Television: From Cop Shows to Cartoons in American Culture*. New York: Routledge, 2004.

"MPAA Adds New Rating to Warn Audiences of Films Not Based on Existing Works." The Onion 20 Oct. 2015. www.theonion.com/article/mpaa-adds-new-rating -warn-audiences-films-not-base-51651.

Murphy, Mekado. "They Remade 'Raiders of the Lost Ark.' Here's Why." *New York Times* 8 June 2016.

Musser, Charles. *Before the Nickelodeon: Edwin S. Porter and the Edison Manufacturing Company*. Berkeley: University of California Press, 1991.

Olsen, Mark. "'The Marked Ones' Sequel Provides a Fresh, Fun Fright." *Chicago Tribune* 4 Jan. 2014.

"Paranormal Activity." Box Office Mojo. Accessed 2 Oct. 2016 www.boxofficemojo.com/movies/?id=paranormal activity.htm.

"PBS Announces New Series Inspired by *Mister Rogers' Neighborhood* Character Daniel Tiger." *Business Wire* 31 July 2011.

Plasketes, George. "Introduction: Like a Version." *Play It Again: Cover Songs in Popular Music*. Ed. George Plasketes. Farnham, UK: Ashgate, 2010. 1–7.

Proctor, William. "Interrogating *The Walking Dead*: Adaptation, Transmediality, and the Zombie Matrix." *Remake Television: Reboot, Re-use, Recycle*. Ed. Carlen Lavigne. Lanham, MA: Lexington Books, 2014. 5–20.

———. "Regeneration & Rebirth: An Anatomy of the Franchise Reboot." *Scope: An Online Journal of Film and Television Studies*, no. 22 (February 2012): 1–19. www.nottingham.ac.uk/scope/documents/2012/february-2012/proctor.pdf.

Ryan, Desmond. "Freddy Krueger Doll Sells Like a Real Dream." *Philadelphia Inquirer* 12 Mar. 1989.

Saltzman, Marc. "New 'Batman' Game a Deliciously Dark Adventure." Gannett News Service 27 Aug. 2009.

Santo, Avi. *Selling the Silver Bullet: The Lone Ranger and Transmedia Brand Licensing*. Austin: University of Texas Press. 2015.

Scheuer, Philip K. "Tradition Trampled Upon as Films Revive Classics." *Los Angeles Times* 4 Sept. 1932.

Smith, Iain Robert, and Constantine Verevis. "Introduction: Transnational Film Remakes." *Transnational Film Remakes*. Ed. Iain Robert Smith and Constantine Verevis. Edinburgh: Edinburgh University Press, 2017. 1–18.

Stam, Robert. "The Dialogics of Adaptations." *Film Adaptations*. Ed. James Naremore. New Brunswick, NJ: Rutgers University Press. 54–76.

Thompson, Gary. "'Force Awakens' Is the 'Star Wars' Reboot Fans Wanted." *TCA Regional News* 16 Dec. 2016.

Trachtenberg, Jeffrey, and Ben Fritz. "Media: 'Star Wars' Cloak of Secrecy Covers Books—Publisher Delays 'Force Awakens' in Hardcover to Help Keep Details of Plot under Wraps." *Wall Street Journal* 2 Nov. 2015.

Tryon, Chuck. "Reboot Cinema." *Convergence: The International Journal of Research into New Media Technologies* 19.4 (2013): 423–437.

Van Der Lind, Damon. "A Force to Be Reckoned With: Meet the Woman Creating the Next Star Wars Video Game Empire." *National Post* 21 Nov. 2015.

Verevis, Constantine. *Film Remakes*. Edinburgh: Edinburgh University Press, 2006.

Warner, Kristen J. *The Cultural Politics of Colorblind TV Casting*. New York: Routledge, 2015.

Williams, Raymond. *Keywords: A Vocabulary of Culture and Society*. Rev. ed. New York: Oxford University Press, 1983.

Zeitchik, Steven. "'Star Wars' Plan in Works." *Los Angeles Times* 1 Nov. 2012.

INDEX

Abrams, J. J., 16

actors, 27, 40, 63–64, 99.
See also social diversity in
casts and casting

adaptations: as cultural category, 28–29; cultural status
of sources, 29, 77–78; definition of, 26; different ways
each version tells stories,
28; fidelity to source of,
27–28, 29, 54, 57; as form
of intertextuality, 26; as
intermedial, 26–29; and
process of franchising,
89–90; "readaptations," 74;
ready-made narratives and,
78; of series, 31; series distinguished from, 29, 30; silent
films and, 75–76, 77–78;
slipperiness of term, 49;
specific characteristics of
each medium used in, 27. *See
also* industrial intertextuality; intertextuality, forms of

African Americans. *See* race
and ethnicity, engagement
with

Ain't It Cool News (website),
2–3, 4, 27

Airport series: *Airport* (1970),
37; *Airport 1975* (1974), 37;
Airplane! (1980), 37

Alien vs. Predator: Extinction
(2003), 26

Alien vs. Predator: Extinction
(video game), 26

American Mutoscope and
Biograph (film company),
70–71

*American Mutoscope and
Biograph Co. v. Edison Manufacturing Co.*, 52, 71

America Online (AOL), 65

Amos 'n' Andy (1928–1960;
radio), 31

Amos 'n' Andy (1951–1953; television), 31

Andrew, Dudley, 28

AOL, 65

Arrival of the Train (1897),
67–69

audiences, 6; convergence
and, 43; mental activity of,
as work of industrial

ABOUT THE AUTHOR

Daniel Herbert is an associate professor in the Department of Screen Arts and Cultures at the University of Michigan. He is the author of *Videoland: Movie Culture at the American Video Store* (2014) as well as numerous essays about film and media culture.